THE RUSSIAN REVOLUTION, 1917–1945

THE RUSSIAN REVOLUTION, 1917–1945

Anthony D'Agostino

 PRAEGER

AN IMPRINT OF ABC-CLIO, LLC
Santa Barbara, California • Denver, Colorado • Oxford, England

Copyright 2011 by Anthony D'Agostino

All rights reserved. No part of this publication may be reproduced, stored in a retrieval system, or transmitted, in any form or by any means, electronic, mechanical, photocopying, recording, or otherwise, except for the inclusion of brief quotations in a review, without prior permission in writing from the publisher.

Library of Congress Cataloging-in-Publication Data

D'Agostino, Anthony.
   The Russian revolution, 1917–1945 / Anthony D'Agostino.
      p. cm.
   Includes bibliographical references and index.
   ISBN 978-0-313-38622-0 (hard copy : alk. paper) — ISBN 978-0-313-38623-7 (ebook)
1. Soviet Union—History—Revolution, 1917–1921. 2. Soviet Union—History—1917–1936. 3. Soviet Union—History—1925–1953. 4. World War, 1939–1945—Soviet Union. 5. Soviet Union—Politics and government. 6. Social change—Soviet Union—History. I. Title.
DK266.3.D34   2011
947.084′2—dc22   2010037074

ISBN: 978-0-313-38622-0
EISBN: 978-0-313-38623-7

15 14 13 12 11   1 2 3 4 5

This book is also available on the World Wide Web as an eBook.
Visit www.abc-clio.com for details.

Praeger
An Imprint of ABC-CLIO, LLC

ABC-CLIO, LLC
130 Cremona Drive, P.O. Box 1911
Santa Barbara, California 93116-1911

This book is printed on acid-free paper ∞

Manufactured in the United States of America

Contents

Preface

This is a concise introduction to the Russian revolution from 1917 to 1945, that is, in the period prior to the Cold War. Its premise is that the perspectives of the post-1945 period are not adequate to understand the international setting of the revolution in World War I, the Great Depression, and the rise of fascism. Indeed for the Western democracies to think in Cold War terms in those circumstances would at the worst have implied making common cause with the fascists against the "Jewish Bolshevik menace." To say this is not necessarily to imply a critique of the Cold War, but merely to recognize the special demands of international life in the time before the world was divided between East and West. So the book has to account for the irony that, despite the Soviet regime's revolutionary ideology and its internal horrors, it proved to be the valued ally of the Western democracies in their great time of trial and the main factor in the world's salvation from Nazism.

The subject has taken on a different kind of relevance since the end of the Cold War. The Soviet Bloc and Soviet Communism are no more. We now have to ask whether the Russian revolution was a wretched excess of history, a ghoulish detour from the main line of progressive development, or if it may have served some necessary function in producing the world we live in, as we might say of the English revolution of the seventeenth century, the French revolution of the eighteenth, the American revolutionary war for independence, and the struggles of other nations for national self-determination. Instead of viewing the Russian revolution as a preparation for strategic and geopolitical conflict with the United States, I will attempt to explore the issues in the context of the period and its own special problems: the transformation and modernization of the Tsarist Russian state, the World War of

1914–1918, the revolutionary project of Soviet Communism, its nationalist transformation under international pressures, the "Big Drive" to modernize Russia by force, the external threat of fascism, and the evolution of a Soviet regime based both on unremitting terror and a realist foreign policy. The book seeks answers to four questions: Why did the Tsarist regime unravel in revolution? Why did the Bolsheviks come to power rather than some other party, specifically the liberal Constitutional Democrat (Kadet) party or the peasant party of the Socialist Revolutionaries, both of which might have entertained realistic hopes to lead a Russian democracy? Why did Stalin, rather than some other more popular, more respected leader, win the mantle of Lenin and leadership of the ruling party? How must the Stalin regime, with its ghastly internal tyranny and its war against Nazism, be judged by subsequent generations of Russians and by world history?

Since the fall of Soviet Communism in 1991, Russians have been asking these questions anew, wondering if the revolution of Gorbachev and Yeltsin has succeeded in affecting a "synchronization of our social clock with the West," in the phrase used by an authoritative post-Soviet textbook for Russian high school students. Despite everything, the authors retain a vast pride in the "heroism, self-sacrifice, and military strength" on display in the events that will be described in this volume. Would these qualities have been less without the revolution? Can they be ascribed instead to a Russian national idea? It may be that these are questions that will come into better focus with the perpective we now enjoy.

One might begin by asking where the Tsarist regime and state were headed in the period before the revolution. Was Russia evolving politically and socially or just getting stronger? Romanov Russia might be compared with other modernizing old regimes, Hohenzollern Germany, Habsburg Austria, and Meiji Japan. Austria collapsed in World War I. Germany and Japan became fascist regimes. Was Russia saved by the revolution from following down one of these paths? After 1917 Soviet Russia issued a call for the "overthrow of the existing cosmos," according to British Home Secretary Oliver Joynson-Hicks's colorful phrase. The Bolsheviks assumed the revolution would spread by way of Germany, France, and Western countries where the urban proletariat was active politically. Why then did this call resonate at first primarily in the world outside Europe, in Turkey, Persia, China, and India? Was the failure of the world revolution the key to the rise of Stalin, as his rival Trotsky later argued? Or was Stalin the beneficiary of the inherent problems of succession in a dictatorship? Lenin could hardly have supposed in 1917 that his party would undertake the industrialization of Russia. But that was what it eventually did. How did this happen? Many studies take the view that the Stalin regime was inherent in Leninism. But why, then, did Stalin end up executing the entire generation of Lenin's comrades? On the other hand, we can hardly deny that Stalin considered himself the best pupil of Lenin.

When the American president Franklin Roosevelt recognized Russia in 1933, Soviet commentators interpreted the act as one flowing from the joint interest of Russia and the United States in containing Japan's expansion in the Far East. Could revolutionary Russia, even under the leadership of Stalin about to embark on the great purges, still have state interests in common with one of the most progressive Western states? If so, could one say that there was a Russian or Soviet national interest that transcended the revolutionary project? The heroism of Soviet history that enjoys such a celebration among Soviet and post-Soviet historians refers to the period of the five-year plans and to the Great Patriotic War against Nazi Germany. Could the Soviet people have accomplished these great deeds without Stalin? If not, does that make him the greatest hero of Soviet/Russian history?

In his campaign for glasnost in 1987, Gorbachev intended that serious answers be given to all these questions, which up to then had only been attempted in Western literature or in the potted Stalinist rewrite of 1938, *The History of the Communist Party of the Soviet Union (Bolshevik): Short Course*. A start was made, but Gorbachev and the glasnost press soon went directly to the question of how to terminate the revolution and the Soviet state. So Russia has not really come to accounts with its Soviet past and the agenda of de-Stalinization.

Now we see the reverse process. Russians are no longer reacting with shame to the memory of the Stalin years. They find in him a symbol of Russian greatness and an inspiration in their attempt to overcome what Vladimir Putin has called the greatest geopolitical disaster in history, the partition of the Soviet Union. The revival of National Bolshevism, Russian National Socialism, and the related ideological outpourings are not merely the affair of fringe parties. The rebirth of what the Russian philosopher Nikolai Berdyaev called the Russian Idea is also a stated aim of the ruling party, United Russia, and Vladimir Putin and Dmitry Medvedev as well. When Russian nationalists separate Stalin from Communism and put him into the Byzantine iconostasis with their saints and national heroes they mix up historical questions with a lot of dubious national mysticism. The world is watching them with trepidation.

I would hope that it would still be of use to them and to the world to restate the issues of the time of Russia's greatest agony soberly in the terms of the period itself, terms that were understandable to the whole world, and especially to America, with rational parameters, indulging neither the excesses of the worst of the nightmares of the Cold War era nor the fantasies of a messianic Russian nationalism.

China still calls itself Communist, along with North Korea, Vietnam, Cuba, and mass movements in Nepal, India, and other places. The rest of us might ask what Communism was or is. Was it really a regime of nationalism, having the main function of bolstering the state? If one considers that idea, does one say that socialism in the last analysis is not the emancipatory project of the proletariat, but of the intelligentsia, the managing and superintending class of all modern societies? If we add to that consideration of the obvious choice the Russian intelligentsia made for the market in 1989–1991, have we admitted the truth of one wag's line during the glasnost era, to the effect that "Communism is the longest and most painful transition to capitalism"? Study of the Russian revolution has always involved a civics lesson. After the end of Soviet power, it still does, except that the lesson needs to be redefined.

This book tries to raise all the most important questions and to out-line some of the different positions historians have taken. And I have offered some of my own interpretations, in the spirit of a short intro-duction. Considering this task I remembered a story told about Lenin, no doubt quite apocryphal, giving advice to a young person about how to study a foreign language. Lenin is supposed to have said, "Start with memorizing all the nouns, then the verbs, then the adjectives, adverbs, prepositions, conjunctions, etc." A short introduction can set for its task the exposition of essential facts and dates, the building blocks one needs before one takes on the big issues. But if it must indeed be short, it should try to connect these to issues and lines of argument. Better, I have decided, to lay out major points of contro-versy, even if arguments cannot be exhausted the way they might be in a larger volume. In attempting this I realize that I have left out a good deal of important subject matter, not only areas to which I could not do justice within the scope of the enterprise but also essential background and detail for the questions I do take up.

I have not written with the expectation that this is the last book the reader will ever consult on the subject nor that mine will be the last word. The interested reader coming to the subject for the first time will have to consult other works to go further. The suggestions for further reading at the end of the book are not intended to account for everything available in a field that is highly productive, especially now that new materials are being used by scholars. I have not gone beyond indicating the first echelon of works that the student can consult to read his or her way into the subject. In most cases the suggestions are confined to material most readily accessible to the English language reader. The assumption is that the student can learn from a great many works with different perspectives and approaches, even if the authors may not be on speaking terms. This has certainly been my experience. It is all the more regrettable that many works of value could not be included. I have tried to range over the decades of literature on this subject and cite classics, revisionist works, curiosities, and work done during and since the Gorbachev years. For transliteration of Russian names, while the Library of Congress is the base, every possible concession has been made to familiarity. Thus Leon Trotsky rather than Lev Trotskii; Zinoviev rather than Zinov'ev.

I should thank some colleagues, friends, and students who helped with the enterprise in one way or another. Peter Gray, Werner Hahn, and Jonathan Harris read the manuscript and gave me the benefit of their thoughts, not all of which, it should go without saying, were identical to mine. I also benefitted from the reaction to specific chapters of Jacob Boas and Kathryn Lenhart. Michael Millman did everything that a patient and understanding editor might do, and a good deal more. To these and others I express my gratitude for the opportunity to engage in dialogue about these burning issues long past.

CHAPTER 1

Land and People

The Russian revolution can be said to have its origin at the confluence of two historical streams: the rising power of the imperial Russian state and the idealism of the Western socialist movement. We begin our inquiry with a consideration of the first stream, that is, of the peculiar character of Russia's political institutions and the unique features of its imperial expansion.

The greatest and best loved of the prerevolutionary Russian historians, Vasilii Kliuchevskii, called Russian history a tale of peoples in movement, which he told in terms of an alternance of invasion, defeat, victory, and finally expansion. Kliuchevskii was generalizing about the settlement of Russia and of the movement of Turko-Mongol tribes across Russia's inviting steppe roads (actually not so different from the movement of barbarian tribes across Western Europe, 300–800 A.D.). He was also taking note of Russia's later interaction with settled and civilized states such as Sweden and Poland, whose invasions were each repelled by a Russian national rally. The story of Napoleon and Hitler in Russia thus fits a certain well-worn pattern.

Geographic factors have usually been cited to help explain this Russian vulnerability to invasion, particularly that Russia had no large mountain barriers such as the Alps or the Pyrenees. The Urals, considered the boundary between Europe and Asia since the time of Peter the Great, have always been easily crossed. Scholars who study prehistory tell us that, in general, cultural diffusion takes place more easily along an east-west axis than a north-south. Movement along similar latitudes is more likely than movement into different ones. Russia has four distinct latitudinal zones of climate and vegetation. At the extremes of north and south are tundra and desert. The two

1

middle belts are forest and steppe (prairie). George Vernadsky, dean of the "Eurasian school" of historians and philologists that emerged in the 1920s, argued that Russia's history could be viewed as a struggle between the forest and the steppe, with one dominating and then giving way to the other. Steppe peoples sweep across settled areas and hold sway for a time, but they have great difficulty penetrating and holding the lands of the forest peoples. We will consider this as we review the succession of Russian state forms. Along with the thesis of the conflict of forest and steppe goes that of the river roads and Russia's presumed "Drive to the Sea." The cities and towns of European Russia were first settled along the great river roads, including the Dvina, the Volkhov, the Volga, and the Dnieper. Villages and towns were also founded at portages between river systems where migrants built the first forts (*ostrogi*). Harsh extremes of climate have impressed European visitors and given rise to theorizing about pre-sumed effects on the Russian character, said to be mercurial and unpredictable. In the 1950s much was made of characterological explanations of the mysteries of Soviet behavior in world politics. The anthropologist Goeffrey Gorer even found the key to Russian xenophobia in the swaddling of babies, which, he thought, restricted the Russian personality.

Should we think of Russia as belonging to Europe or Asia? The Greek historian Herodotus spoke of the lands north of the Black Sea as those of the Scythians and Sarmatians. For him, Sarmatia Asiatica and Sarmatia Europea divided at the Bosporus. In Asian terms it may be convenient to consider the state that rose around Moscow between the thirteenth and sixteenth centuries as one of the "gun-powder empires," alongside Safavid Persia, Mughal India, and Ming China. In European terms one thinks of Russia as a vast hinterland on the world island extending from the little cape of Europe. Through Russia, Europe looks out to Asia. Looking from Europe to Russia also means confronting a dilution of Western institutional patterns. As the Russian Marxist and later Liberal Pëtr Struve put it, "The further east one goes the more sparse the population, the harder the climate, the weaker, the more cowardly and abject does the bourgeoisie become politically and the more do its cultural and political tasks devolve upon the proletariat." This thought, in its various forms and expressions, about which we will say more below, was the point of departure for the revolutionary speculations about the future of Russia that were finally given a platform by the revolutions of 1917.

The first Russian state, say the Russians, was Kiev *Rus* on the Dnieper River road to Byzantium, "from the Vikings to the Greeks," a state founded by Norsemen, according to the eighteenth-century German philologists Bayer and Schlözer. At any rate, so say some, but not all, Russian historians. Was *Rus* a word for Russia? Russian historians have thought so. For most of them, *Rossiia* denotes the lands and peoples of Great Russia, Ukraine, and Belarus, but Kiev Rus was the ancestor of the Muscovite state. Professor Vernadsky moreover insisted that *Rus* is a word in the language of the Alans, an ancient steppe people. Even the Russian word for God, *Bog*, is said to be an Alanic word, still more indication that Russia is Eurasian. Aleksandr Blok, the greatest Soviet poet, reminded the world of that claim when he addressed Western Europe in 1918 in his *Scythians*:

> Of you there are millions.
> Of us—hordes and hordes and hordes
> Just try to match your strength with us!
> Yes, we are Scythians. Yes, we are Asiatics,
> With slant and avaricious eyes!

Others, especially Polish scholars and Ukrainian nationalists, insist that Kiev *Rus* should not be thought of as a precursor to Muscovy. "Ruthenian" is, according to them, the only way to translate *Rus*. The name of the present Soviet successor state, Belarus, with its capital at Minsk, is no longer translated as "Belorussia," in a seeming assertion of the idea that *Rus* is not Russia. In this perspective, the first Russian state in the Ukraine was not Russian at all. Yet much of Russian institutional life begins there. The Christian baptism of *Rus* in the eastern orthodox rite committed the country to a cultural link with Byzantium rather than Western Europe. From Byzantium comes the Russian conception of autocratic power and its symbol in the double eagle, as well as the unity of church and state as found in Byzantine Caesaro-Papism. The contrast with Western Latin conceptions of a division of church and state was obvious and painful to nineteenth-century intellectuals such as Pëtr Chaadayev, who lamented that Russia had not been baptized by Rome and attached to the mainstream of Western culture. Chaadayev was one of the first non-Marxist writers to enjoy a vogue when intellectual life was opened up under Gorbachev and the glasnost campaign in 1987. On the other side, historians such as Leopold von Ranke and Henri Pirenne, citing the good trade contacts and intermarriage with central European royal families, have denied that Byzantine Christianity ever cut off Kiev *Rus* from the West.

At any rate, the steppe conquerors broke the Kievan contacts with Byzantium and doomed the state to decline and disappearance, beginning with the invasions of the Pechenegs (tenth and eleventh centuries) and the Polovtsy (eleventh to thirteenth centuries) and ending with the greatest steppe conquerors, the Mongols, in the thirteenth century. In Vernadsky's terms, the steppe had conquered the forest. Reorientation of trade from the river roads to the Mediterranean was further influenced by the Crusades and the subsequent rise of the Italian city-states. The Mongols broke the Kievan state into independent principalities, for which the term *appanages* was used by French writers in the nineteenth century. The Polish-Lithuanian state founded in the fourteenth century eventually absorbed White Ruthenia and Ukraine. *Rossiia* was divided and for several centuries Russian *appanage* princes paid tribute either to the Swedes, the Poles, or, in most cases, to the Mongol khans.

When a new power emerged around the Duchy of Muscovy in the twelfth century, it was at first a most faithful servitor of the Mongols. As Muscovy rose up fitfully against the Mongols in the fourteenth and fifteenth centuries it also conquered Novgorod and other northern towns. Nineteenth-century intellectuals thought of this as another cultural tragedy. The northern city-states were linked to Lithuania and to the Baltic trade of the Hanseatic League and were taken to be little germs of a westernized commercial life that could have connected Russians to the centers of civilized existence, instead of dark and primitive Muscovy. In 1480 Muscovy formally declared its independence of what later historians called the "Mongol Yoke." In Vernadsky's terms, the forest had struck back against the steppe. Ivan the Third, "the Great" (1462–1505), was the first to refuse tribute. It is worth noting that he was a contemporary of Henry the Seventh of England, who also took a key step toward building a territorial state when he prohibited "maintenance and livery," that is, private armies. So Muscovy and England, not to mention France and Spain, could be said to have arisen as states at roughly the same time. Ivan the Fourth, "The Terrible" (1533–1584), who thought about marrying Queen Elizabeth (to her horror), took the next step by leading Russian armies down the Volga to win Kazan and Astrahan. Ivan failed, however, in attempting to extend Russian power to the Baltic coast. Russia still lacked access to the Baltic or the Black Sea. That expansion was to be the work of Peter the Great (1672–1796) and Catherine the Great (1729–1796).

In this early period one can already see the development of a characteristic and peculiar institutional relationship between crown and nobility. In the history of every European state this relationship is central. With the rise of absolute monarchy, the nobility sought to defend their traditional dues and ward off new taxes by means of parliaments.

A constitution, as came into being in England and Poland, was a sign of noble victory, while an unlimited "New Monarchy," as in Spain, France, or Russia, marked its defeat. The money economy that spread explosively when Western Europeans began to ply the Atlantic made the New Monarchies possible and also divided the nobility into classes. Impoverished nobles were driven into various adventures: Protestantism and wars over the church lands for the German knights, colonial conquest for the hidalgoes in Spain, commercial agriculture for the English gentry. The Russian gentry's adventure was absolute monarchy. In Russia the crown made the gentry its servitor class. The losers were the aristocratic and constitutionally minded nobility, defeated more completely than in any other European state. By the eighteenth century, when some of Russia's titled intellectuals began to ponder this historical legacy, there arose a critique of serfdom and an enthusiasm for Western ideas. These never produced any constitutionalist movement. In the nineteenth century Alexis de Tocqueville and the English Whig historians underlined the now commonplace reflection that the historic basis of all freedom was the freedom of the nobility. On that account, Russia must be judged, and was judged, the worst tyranny in Europe.

The perceived contrast between Western freedom and Russian tyranny may have been bolstered by the emerging European division of labor during the time of the rise of the tsars. If we imagine a line through the center of Europe roughly tracing Churchill's Iron Curtain, from Szeczin to Trieste, we can say that by 1500 the area to the west of this line had seen the near disappearance of serfdom, whereas the area to the east of it saw after 1500 the gradual *imposition* of serfdom, called by historians the "second serfdom." Overseas commerce enriched the western towns; peasants became freemen; shipbuilding and urban growth created new demands for timber and grain. These were needed in the west and produced in the east. And on the estates of the East European countries, peasants had to be prohibited from running off to settle the vast lands to their east and south, and this was done by the imposition of serfdom. In Poland the gentry suppressed the merchantry politically and dominated the grain trade down the Vistula. In Russia the gentry produced for a domestic market and owed their control over the serfs to their own service to the crown.

One can see some benchmarks for all these trends in the reign of Ivan the Terrible. The first trading contact with England was established. The peasantry's movement was increasingly restricted. Ivan terrorized the aristocratic Boyars with his *oprichnina*, a campaign of violent official oppression and murder. It was said of the *oprichniki* that they rode the countryside with a dog's head and a broom, to symbolize their dog-like loyalty to the tsar and their mission to sweep the country clean of his enemies. An unfinished poem, *Kakaya Noch!* (What a Night!) by Aleksandr Pushkin tells of an *oprichnik* riding across Red Square past corpses and other evidences of the horrors of the previous day, whose horse, but not he, is visibly shocked at the sight. The poem expresses a reaction of shame on the part of the nineteenth century intelligentsia confronting the Russian past.

By an edict of 1649, serfdom was more or less complete. Russia had arrived at a terrible bargain that has been described by historian Richard Pipes as a kind of dyarchy, stipulating that the tsar would dominate the nobles and the nobles would dominate the peasantry. Historians have found this relationship to be the centerpiece of Russian history. Kliuchevskii spoke of the "manorial-dynastic conception of the state," and art historian Vladimir Weidlé wrote of "a vertical state ruling a horizontal society." This view has been put more strongly: it has been asserted that Russia experienced no constitutional tradition, no Magna Carta, no medieval town charters or free universities, no Renaissance, no Reformation, no Enlightenment. All this according to the best Western political thought.

Yet the cruel conditions in Russia were not entirely unique. In Poland the nobles won their contest with the crown. The Polish gentry (*szlachta*) got a constitution that permitted them to dominate parliamentary life and elect the monarch. Nevertheless, they still imposed serfdom on the peasantry. And their constitution did not provide much of a defense of the security of their state. It gave each delegate to the parliament, the *Sejm*, a liberum veto, a free veto that would not only kill any proposed law but also "explode" the *Sejm* itself. In the eighteenth century, as the time approached for Poland to defend its territorial integrity against the rising power of Prussia, Austria, and Russia, she found herself defenseless against partition and disappearance as a state. It might be said that the very freedom of the *szlachta*, what has been called the "szlachta democracy," contributed to the loss of Polish statehood.

Moreover, Russia certainly did not invent absolute monarchy. Ivan the Terrible was a contemporary of Henry the Eighth. As for the domestication of the Russian gentry, French absolute monarchy also depended on a *noblesse de la robe* that was as much a court nobility as the Russian *dvorianstvo* (from the word for court, *dvor*). To be sure, Russia's tyranny was more grinding and in many ways more thoroughgoing. By the time of Peter the Great, the servitor gentry had in effect been transformed into a state bureaucracy according to an official Table of Ranks. Nobles continued to hold their lands by virtue of service to the state. It was possible for some Europeans to see Russia as Karl Marx did, as a species of oriental despotism arising out of an "Asiatic mode of production." When one considers that, for Marx, this was a stage prior to antiquity, one gets a new appreciation of the Western hyperbole of Russian backwardness.

But along with this goes Voltaire's contrary thought that monarchy, and especially the absolute monarchy of Peter the Great, was necessary to the survival of the Russian state. Voltaire was an admirer of Enlightened Despotism, which he thought might be efficacious in the West. But even Montesquieu, who rejected the idea, nevertheless cautioned that only a geographically small country could enjoy a polity of virtue. Russian historians such as S. F. Platonov have admired Ivan the Terrible precisely for his defense of the Russian state power against domestic and foreign opponents.

At least by the time of Peter the Great Russia had become part of a European international system governed by ideas of a balance of power. At the end of the seventeenth century, while Britain sought various ways to balance the power of Louis the Fourteenth of France, in the same way that she had earlier tried to balance Spanish power, Russia sent Cossack communities into Siberia to ply its river roads in search of furs. At the same time she sought ways to expand at the expense of Sweden, Poland, Turkey, and Persia. All of these were themselves expanding powers. Swedish and Polish troops had invaded Russia during the Time of Troubles, the period of domestic chaos prior to the establishment of the Romanov dynasty. In 1654 a Cossack revolt brought the Ukraine out of Polish hands and attached it to Russia. While the great European powers were engaged in the War of Spanish Succession at the turn of the eighteenth century, Russia was involved in a protracted war with Sweden, decided finally by the defeat of the brilliant Swedish king Charles the Twelfth, at Poltava in the Ukraine. Peter the Great was thus able to win Swedish lands on the Baltic coast, where he built his capital, Saint Petersburg.

The balance of power that checked the rivals of the British in Western Europe had an eastern mechanism that promoted Russian growth. While the British looked to Austria and Prussia to balance France, Russia also looked to them to weaken the French friends Sweden, Poland, and Ottoman Turkey. Curiously, Britain and Russia saw the balance of power in much the same way. Up to the time of Napoleon, Britain generally looked with favor on Russian success against the potential allies of France. Catherine managed to extend Russia to the Black Sea, as Peter had the Baltic, winning the Crimea from the Ottoman Empire. She joined with Austria and Prussia to partition Poland and remove it from the map. It would not return until 1918. The gradual decline of the power of the Ottoman Empire after the failure of its siege of Vienna in 1683 made it possible for Russia to make war against it almost constantly. Russian policy would be more and more obsessed with the desire to possess or control the straits between the Mediterranean and the Black Seas, the Bosporus and the Dardanelles, to make Russia a power in the Mediterranean. The French revolution and the Napoleonic wars worked to Russia's advantage as they did to the British with their four coalitions against France. While the British reinforced their hold on Gibraltar and gathered in Malta, the Ionian Islands, the Cape of Good Hope, and Ceylon, the Russians collected Finland and the Åland Islands, Bessarabia, Georgia, Armenia, and Azerbaijan. Then Russia defeated Napoleon's invasion and made herself the arbiter of European politics well into the nineteenth century, intervening in 1849 to keep Hungary from winning its independence from Austria.

By this time two generations of British leaders had reversed the earlier favorable view of Russian expansion. Previously they had thought that Russian quarrels with Sweden made their own access to the Baltic easier; similarly Russo-Turkish wars made less likely a combination preventing their access to the eastern Mediterranean. After the defeat of Napoleon, however, they came to see Russian impositions on the Ottoman Empire as a menace, under the rubric of what they liked to call the "Eastern Question," that is, the question of how to stop Russia. As badly as Russia wanted control over the Straits, Britain sought to deny them to her. What was more, Britain's interest in the matter appeared wholesome to many who thought at least some of the ideas of the Enlightenment and the French revolution to be progressive and who had to regard expansionist Russia as the most reactionary state in Europe. When Britain and France made war on Russia in the Crimea (1853–1856), Karl Marx called on the British workers to support the military campaigns of their government. The cause of the workers, he said, and the struggle against Russia were one and the same.

After her defeat by Britain and France in the Crimean War, Russia turned away from the Near Eastern Question. Prince Aleksandr Gorchakov, Chancellor to the Russian Empire in the reign of Aleksandr the Second, urged that Russia leave the Near East to Britain and France for a time, allow them to indulge their natural quarrels, while she concentrated on internal reform and expansion toward areas of low political pressure. The Tsar Liberator abolished serfdom. Russia advanced in Central Asia and the Far East in the 1860s and 1870s.

Taking advantage of the indisposition of China after the Taiping rebellion, she absorbed territories in the Amur River valley and founded the port city of Vladivostok. At the end of the nineteenth century, with the rise of a possibly friendly Germany, expansionists thought that this would have been crowned by winning the Dardanelles and Bosporus and making Russia a genuinely Mediterranean power. Desire to take the Straits lay at the root of her involvement in the crises in the Near East in the 1870s and 1880s, and the Balkan wars of 1912–1913. And this in turn was related to Russian defense of Serbia in 1914, which dragged her into the war that finally tore her apart. Russia was not only the most grinding tyranny in Europe but also one of its most aggressive imperial powers, at a time when Social Darwinist imperialism dominated the viewpoint of all the Western powers.

How do we sum up the problem of Russia and the West? Russia had no free nobility, no self-conscious and vigorous civil society, no constitution, and no experience of civic revolution as with Holland in the sixteenth century, Britain in the seventeenth, or France or America in the eighteenth. Russian opinion was acutely aware, therefore, that its dramatic expansion as an imperial power was viewed with the greatest trepidation by progressive and liberal Europe. Thinking Russians perceived inferiority along what historian Theodore Von Laue has called the "cultural slope" of the great powers, a slope that indicates both political power and cultural sophistication. Some great internal renovation would be necessary to move up the cultural slope.

In response to this perceived gap in standards of civilization, back in the time of Peter the Third, in 1762, the crown had freed the nobility from service, without, however, freeing the peasants from serfdom. In the nineteenth century the Russian literary critic Mikhailovskii suggested that the "conscience-stricken nobleman" had first appeared among the ranks of liberated gentry with a burden of guilt over this circumstance and a desire to compensate by seeking political and social change, even change that was thought revolutionary in nature. Russia was to be made a civilized country by internal transformation. This, it was thought, was the mission of the Russian intelligentsia.

CHAPTER 2

The Intelligentsia and the West

T he revolution that shook the world in 1917 had by that time been stirring in the minds of Russian intellectuals for at least a century. Radical notions of liberalism, democracy, socialism, and anarchism did not spring spontaneously from the workers and the peasants, those groups among the people whom they were said to benefit, but from the *intelligentsiia*. This is a Russian noun from the middle of the nineteenth century used to denote intellectuals. The entry for *intelligentsiia* in a prerevolutionary encyclopedia would also include, alongside a definition of an intellectual—one who thinks deeply about religion and social life, who interests oneself in philosophical rumination, who appreciates the arts, music, dance—an important additional idea: one who opposes the government. In Soviet-era encyclopedias, however, these ideas no longer appear. Instead we find something different: administrative and technical personnel, professionals, white-collar workers and civil servants, those whose work entails managing and superintending, those engaged in intellectual rather than physical labor.

Does the difference between the two definitions tell the story of a social transformation wrought by the Russian revolution? Can we say that the modern white-collar class had its origin among the various gentry intellectuals and *raznochintsy* ("men of all ranks") who speculated on the perfection of society in the nineteenth century? Or, should we say that an economic definition of the modern intelligentsia was something that could only be guessed at before the revolution? Along with their ruminations about the society of the future the revolutionary intellectuals themselves devoted no little time to an attempt to address these matters, an effort at self-consciousness in the form of the question: What is the intelligentsia?

The first representatives of the intelligentsia are said to have emerged at the end of the eighteenth century during the reign of Catherine the Great, a time when Russia's attempt to establish herself as an equal of the European powers gave rise to feverish debates about Russia and the West. Peter the Great had admired the maritime nations and wanted Russia to be more like them. In the eighteenth century this meant being more like the French; for Catherine it meant planting the seeds of a Russian version of the French Enlightenment. She was flattered by the fashionable Western notion of "enlightened despotism." But the outbreak of the French revolution threw her into reverse. She wanted no imitation on Russian soil. Russian critics such as Aleksandr Radishchev, who described serfdom as an impediment to cultural advance, found themselves regarded and treated as subversives.

Yet the mood of the court in the years of the mobilization against Napoleon's invasion was favorable to some kind of constitutional experiment and the reform, if not to the abolition of, serfdom. Defeat of Napoleon inspired enthusiasm among the Russian notables for further advance in Russia's modernization. For them this could only mean advance according to Western models, in the event, according to the ideas of the French revolution. This could be seen in some of the reform plans submitted to Tsar Aleksandr the First. The plans never bore fruit because of the mood of the post-Napoleonic era and a general conservative desire to suppress the reverberations of the revolution all over Europe. Russia was thought by the other powers the last line of protection; to European radicals she would become known as the gendarme of Europe. However, on the death of the tsar in December 1825, some army officers staged a rising designed to dictate the succession and bring some vast new change to the country. The Decembrist revolt might be seen as nothing more than a manifestation of Russia's tradition of palace revolution. The first decades of the seventeenth century, the "Era of the Guards," had seen a number of garrison revolts affecting the succession. But Decembrism was a bit more in that it echoed the programs of the French revolution, in effect the only language of liberation available to it. The officers who led it had been in Paris after defeating Napoleon. They found that they admired some of the social and cultural aspects of the revolution and wished to bring Russia abreast of them. The programs of the Decembrist secret societies show a French spectrum of political opinion. Nikita Muraviev's Northern Society adhered to a Whig-Girondin model of constitutional monarchy, and the Southern society, led by Pavel Pestel, to a radical Jacobin-democratic one.

The revolt was suppressed and nothing more was heard of its ideas and programs for a generation. Yet study groups and secret societies continued to dream about changing Russia. In the 1830s and 1840s opposed schools of Slavophils and Westerners debated the future Russian relation to the West. Should Russia strive to emulate Western institutions and ideas? Should it learn from German philosophy and a French Enlightenment tradition of thought that seemed to lead naturally to democracy and socialism? Or should it, as the Slavophils thought, reject even the modernizing heritage of Peter the Great and oppose any project for change as fatal to Russia's unique sense of spiritual community? Out of this debate came a fateful contribution, the liberal critic Aleksandr Herzen's suggestion, in a letter of 1851 to the French nationalist historian Jules Michelet, that a Russian revolution might actually deepen society's organic unity and happiness. A traditional rural institution (or so it was thought), the repartitional commune, the *mir*, could be a possible point of departure for a revolutionary reorganization that would permit Russia to escape the misery and class conflict that industrialization had brought the West. Russia would skip industrial capitalism and find its way to an agrarian socialism expressing her unique genius. Herzen's idea was to be the centerpiece of the movement of Russian populism, *narodnichestvo*, from *narod*, the people or the nation. The populist idea was to drive a movement that would hold center stage among the radical intelligentsia into the twentieth century.

Russia's defeat in the Crimean War, 1853–1856, exposed the weakness of the empire and prompted an attempt at renovation in response. Tsar Aleksandr the Second initiated an extraordinary series of reforms, abolishing serfdom and laying the groundwork on the countryside for an institution of self-government in the rural *zemstvo* and a unified legal system. Yet, as the "Tsar-Liberator" was carrying out a program that touched virtually every side of the life of the country, Russian democrats became even more entrenched in their radicalism. The democrats of the 1860s did their best to keep abreast of socialist and anarchist ideas in the West, but they usually gave them a Russian spin. Nikolai Chernyshevsky and Nikolai Dobroliubov read Marx and were impressed by the Marxist political economy. But they read it mostly as a cautionary tale indicating the horrors in store if capitalism should take root in Russia. They were disappointed to find that Marxism envisioned a social revolution only at the end of a lengthy period of capitalist development. They considered political and social revolution as stark alternatives rather than moments in a historical sequence. They disdained and feared a mere political revolution that would bring a bourgeois constitution and a parliament and would prevent, in their view, a real emancipation of the people.

They had a good deal in common with Western anarchists. By the 1860s the greatest figure among the latter was a Russian nobleman, Mikhail Bakunin. He had taken part in the western revolutions of 1848, had been arrested and imprisoned, finally turned over to the Russian government, and exiled to Siberia. He had escaped and shipped out to Yokohama, then to San Francisco, New York, and London in 1861. He was no longer a Pan-Slav as he had been when he was arrested in Germany in 1849. He went to Italy and tried to find a way to relate to the political life of the Italian Risorgimento. He finally did so as an apostle of anarchism, propaganda for which he helped spread all over Europe. His anarchism was based on the idea of workers in trade unions as the leaders of a new stateless society. He believed that anarchists ought not to limit themselves to propaganda but should also organize the labor movement. By the turn of the century, this creed became known as anarcho-syndicalism and enjoyed considerable success in France and Spain. But for Russia, he could not embrace populism according to the idea of the *mir*. He did preach the great Russian jacquerie in the style of the French peasant war, the "Great Fear" of 1789.

Bakunin wanted to set the Russian tradition of peasant jacqueries against the traditions of the intelligentsia. He thought he saw a class antagonism within the revolutionary movement. While the intelligentsia fought for a world with a constitution, a new civil order, political freedom, and a career open to the talents, only the people, that is, the peasantry, fought for true liberation according to the old models of Russian *bunt* (riot, tumult, corresponding to the French *émeute*), as seen in the vast jacqueries of Stenka Razin in 1667 and Emelian Pugachëv in 1776. *Narodniki* threw themselves into two attempts at a rebellion of this kind, the "movement to the people" (*khozhdenie v narod*) of 1874 and a smaller rising around Kiev in 1876. These were both quickly suppressed by the alert work of the Tsarist secret police, who took the movement seriously, worked their spies into it, and gained for themselves reliable intelligence about the revolutionaries' plans. Exhausted by the failure of the jacquerie, many of the radicals were forced to search their souls for an alternative to Populism. From this came a turn to a new and specifically Russian Marxism.

This was in the 1880s, after the assassination in 1881 of Aleksandr the Second by a populist sect known as the Peoples' Will who had adopted a program of terror against Tsarist officials. Their crowning act, the killing of the greatest agent of reform in Russian history, marked a culmination of the heyday of Populist revolutionism. A wave of repression and counter-reform was unleashed. Its inspiration was the reactionary Procurator of the Holy Synod under Tsar Aleksandr the Third, Konstantin Pobedonostsev. This formidable personality took the view that there was too much that was new in the world and too much that led the people into corruption, public taverns, for example, where they fell into the hands of "publicans, usurers, and Jews." Under his influence there were new press restrictions, university quotas, and a pervasive anti-Semitism. It had been Pobedonostsev's opinion that the triumph of Western ideas in Russia would not result in the reign of the empty civility of the liberals, but in a new order according to the ideas of Karl Marx, which he claimed to have studied. Ironically, here was a discordant echo of a sentiment most often found among the ranks of the radical intelligentsia, that things had to go one way or the other, grinding tyranny and ignorance or the oceanic jacquerie. *Tertium non datur.*

What did Marx say about the Russian revolution? For him Russia was the most reactionary state in Europe, the lynchpin of the Holy Alliance, the gendarme of Europe, the scourge of the revolutions of 1848. Marx had hoped for a democratic revolution in Prussia, whose first task would have been a war against Russia to liberate Poland and revive it as a state. Marx did not feel the same way about all the lands gathered into Russia in recent times. He did not advocate the national liberation of Caucasian or Far Eastern peoples in the Russian empire. Unlike Poland or Hungary, these were not historic nations. Nor did he see the Czechs as worthy of a movement of national self-determination. How to explain the difference between Bakunin, who thought every language group deserved to determine its own affairs and desired to break all the existing states in the world into their components parts, and Marx with his theory of the progressive nature of the states that the workers would inherit one day? Bakunin's idea was straightforward. Marx's did not have any criterion for judging nationalism beyond history itself.

As to Russia, she could be progressive in Asia, but she was always reactionary in Europe. During the Crimean War, Marx urged the British workers to oppose Russia by supporting their own government. Yet he and Engels suspected the unification of Italy in the Risorgimento to be a Russian and Bonapartist plot. Engels feared the threat to Prussia as a representative of the German national cause. In the 1860s they influenced the International Workingmen's Association to express sympathy for Poland against her Russian oppressors and Ireland against her English ones. In fact they had no rigorous theory of nationalism, but they did believe that the workers, even as "proletarian internationalists," must support the historic nations as they rose up against national oppression. These included Poland, Ireland, and Germany. They had no patience with the argument that nationalism was itself a reactionary and bourgeois idea and that the workers would still be exploited under their national masters. Some theorists, such as the Belgian Cesar de Paepe, came close to saying that. Most anarchists felt the same way. Some of them began to suspect that Marxism as an international revolutionary project only made sense within the framework of the historically specific rise of the new nations of Europe. The rise of the workers internationally would most probably be led by the most vigorous new nation, Germany. That was why Bakunin, while he admired Marx's political economy, still regarded Marxism as bristling with "German" and "Jewish" statist formulations. He put it even more strongly: Marxism, he said, should it ever take power, would introduce the rule, not of the proletariat, but of a new managerial class.

Russian Populists were as eager to have Marx's approval for their revolutionary projects as he was to see the tsar overthrown. While they could hardly say that a Russian agrarian revolution fit the Marxist historical scheme, they nevertheless sent The Teachers frequent letters to get a seal of approval for their work. Was there a place in the Marxist scheme for a revolution based on the village commune? Marx flirted with the idea. He doubted that Russia could avoid capitalism by the route of agrarian socialism. But at the same time he did not want to discourage the Russian revolutionaries and their fight against the Tsar. He had once written that the defeated German revolution of 1848 could only revive in the form of a workers' rising, "backed by a peasant war." Engels told the Jacobin-Blanquist Pëtr Tkachëv in 1874 that an agrarian revolution in Russia might be viable. In 1881 Marx finally wrote in answer to the pleadings of Vera Zasulich that perhaps it might be that agrarian revolution based on the commune could succeed if—the crucial if—it were accompanied by a proletarian revolution in an advanced country. The clouds had parted and the sun shone through on the Russian revolutionaries—or at any rate those who could not live without a sign from Marx. The Russian democratic and agrarian revolution was to be accompanied by the proletarian revolution in Germany. Germany and Russia would be the revolutionary vanguard of humanity. That would be the Marxist formula cited by the Bolsheviks for the revolutionary events of 1917.

Even so, Marx was not entirely happy about the development of a Marxist trend among the Russian exiles in Switzerland in the 1880s. He preferred those populists who carried out attacks on the monarchy to those who were re-thinking populism and considering a turn toward work for a Marxist social democratic party on the German model. Since an industrial working class had not yet appeared, the work of the first Russian Marxists, in the Emancipation of Labor Group led by Georgii Plekhanov, was primarily to produce a learned propaganda rather than to issue calls to action. In that sense the Russian turn to Marxism was a turn to the right.

In the years between the death of Marx in 1883 and that of Engels in 1895, Plekhanov and Engels codified the theory and practice of European Social Democracy and trained the generation of Russian Marxists who would lead the revolution of 1917. In this period the orthodoxy of the later Communist ideology of dialectical materialism was formed and cultivated. It would not be too much to say: no Plekhanov, no Lenin. But at the end of the 1890s conditions changed. Industrialization brought large factories and masses of industrial workers into the Russian cities and with them strikes on a large scale. The Saint Petersburg textile strike of 1896 was the event that signaled a new period. Marxists thought that the time for propaganda had passed and the time for agitation had arrived. According to the old formula of the Populist Tikhomirov, propaganda meant "saying many things to few people," and agitation meant "saying one thing to many people." Alongside the veterans of the old movement there now appeared younger militants such as Martov, Trotsky, and Lenin, who would set it as their task to build a social democratic party and prepare it for the Russian 1789.

Marxists seemed to have won their laborious argument with Populism. "Legal Marxists" made the unanswerable case that capitalism was coming and the country must submit to its hard school. That meant peaceful, legal action, integration of the masses into the life of the nation, and patience for what the future would bring. The Marxist critique of Populism started from the idea that the class on which Populism depended, the peasantry, was in the process of passing from the scene (but not as quickly as one might have thought, as the Soviet Union only reached the point of a majority of urban citizens in the 1950s). By contrast, the class for which the Marxists spoke, the proletariat, advanced in numbers daily with the advent of industrialization. Individual terror therefore made no sense. In general Russia was not to be exceptional. The Russian revolution would advance alongside the Western revolution, that is, probably in the wake of the German revolution. The social democratic parties would work peacefully in democratic politics and throw their energies into the achievement of a "minimum program" of reforms.

The story of the nineteenth-century intelligentsia thus seemed to end with the appearance of Marxism. This is the way we would see it if we were only interested in tracing the antecedents of Bolshevism. We might overlook the fact that Populism was still the idea with the greatest potential for a mass political influence. Under normal conditions, that is, conditions other than war and revolution, the populist idea was bound to be dominant in a country that was more than half peasant until after World War II. However, Russia was not to be given these normal conditions.

Conservative and nationalist intellectuals had said for many decades that Russia would not be permitted to modernize and expand without fierce conflicts with the other imperial powers. The Slavophil Khomiakov had warned that an imperial mission unto brother Slavs of Central and East Central Europe could not be shirked. The poet Tiuchev and the historian Pogodin had argued that the Eastern Question of which the English spoke, the question asking who would liberate the Balkan Slavs from the Ottoman yoke, could be solved only by the Russian Tsar. An ambitious program of Pan-Slavism to accompany the other European Pan movements was issued in 1871 in Nikolai Danilevsky's book, *Russia and Europe*. When Europeans thought about the ideas and aims of Russian imperial policy, they usually invoked Pan-Slavism. Yet there was real fear among Tsarist officials of the effects and possible commitments of the Pan-Slav ideology. The Pan-Slav current among conservative intellectuals only took hold of foreign policy at certain moments of crisis, as during the Russo-Turkish War of 1877. It was always in the air and always part of the estimate of Russian intentions made by the other powers, especially the Germans and the British. The novelist Dostoyevsky insisted that solution of the Eastern Question would also resolve the problem of relations with the West. Russia must spread her wings over Asia and must eclipse Austria in the effort to lead the Balkan Slavs. The cultural slope on which Russia and the West resided and which caused the intelligentsia so much consternation was also a political and military slope. A modernizing and industrializing old regime such as Russia's would not be content with its position for long.

CHAPTER 3

Russia the Modernizing Old Regime

T he years of counter-reform after the assassination of Aleksandr the Second were followed by a period of rapid state-sponsored industrialization aided in large part by foreign capital. State and society underwent a fundamental transformation under the whip of a frenzied international competition for colonies and spheres of influence. Russia continued to look south and east where she saw further opportunities for expansion, but now she carried along dangerous commitments on the European continent as well. Could she maintain her internal equilibrium while contending with the other imperial powers? Russia was living on the edge, yet her leaders were not particularly fearful. Many of the tsar's most able statesmen were thrilled by the prospects and saw great days ahead, hoping that the dynamism of industrialization and rail building would open up new fields for vast endeavors. Along with this went the hope that the broadening context of Russia's quest for power on a world scale would dwarf her social problems. Domestic troubles would be kept in check by foreign policy victories.

Russia may have been the most backward of the great powers, in the sense of undergoing the process of industrial revolution a full century later than Britain and a generation later than Germany, France, and the United States. But her social and political structure was not unique. Along with Hohenzollern Germany, Hapsburg Austria-Hungary, and Meiji Japan, she might be characterized as a modernizing old regime, to be distinguished from Atlantic democracies such as Britain, France, and the United States, nations that had shaped their institutions in revolutions during the seventeenth and eighteenth centuries. The modernizing old regime was an absolute

19

monarchy led by a nobility integrated into national service as the leadership of the officer corps and civil administration. Its bourgeoisie played the leading role in a rapidly developing industry but stayed out of politics. As a modernizing regime, it fostered a large and concentrated force of industrial workers in the cities, whose propensities, one might have supposed at the end of the nineteenth century, would have been toward social democracy. This was the outstanding problem for the modernizing old regime: how to integrate the working class while at the same time warding off the latter's attempts to modernize politically by abolishing absolutism altogether. One solution would have been an authoritarian or fascist state. Three absolute monarchies, Germany, Austria-Hungary, and Russia, perished in World War I. Only Japan survived and thrived under what became a new authoritarianism. This might have been Russia's path under a modernizing absolutism.

States as a rule do not choose their alignments with other states according to affinities of social structure, but according to national interests. Russia might have done both as long as it was connected to Prussia and Austria in the Vienna system of Metternich and later to Germany and Austria-Hungary in Bismarck's League of the Three Emperors (*Dreikaiserbund*). The happy confluence ended when Russia moved away from the eastern monarchies and allied with France in 1894. This fundamental shift in alignment, on which Russia's future would depend, came about almost inadvertently. Tsar Aleksandr wanted more than anything to retain his alliance with Germany and Austria. It was a splendid bloc against the "revolution," in the earlier spirit of the Holy Alliance and the "Vienna system." It was also insurance against the possibility that Poland might rise again, as she had in 1833 and 1863. But Bismarck's Germany was an unreliable partner. Bismarck was too concerned with staying on the good side of the British. When Russia and Turkey tangled over Bosnia in 1878 and war resulted, Bismarck was only too happy to reverse the results of the Russian victory at a European conference. Russia was denied the chance to sponsor Bulgarian independence from the Ottoman Empire. The "Big Bulgaria" that she was attempting to impose on the Turks was taken as possible Russian client state and a threat to spearhead a Russian advance against Constantinople. The Big Bulgaria was subsequently reduced by the agreement of Britain and Germany. The tsar spoke of "a European coalition against Russia under the leadership of Prince Bismarck." This was underlined when Bismarck joined in alliance with Austria in 1879. What could Russia do in response? Turn to France for a counterweight to the Dual Alliance?

The Tsar Liberator shrunk from the thought. France was the spiritual seat of the revolution. After the movements to the people in 1874 and 1876 he realized that Russia was no longer the gendarme of Europe. Now, instead of invading other countries to stamp out the revolution, it was Russia herself that might have to be saved by conservative foreign armies. Both *narodnichestvo* and Pan-Slavism threatened. All Europe seemed to be going to the left. In England, Gladstone brought the Liberals to power in 1880. The French radical Jules Ferry came to power a few months later. Then the Peoples Will carried out the assassination of the Tsar Liberator himself. These multiform threats seemed to impel a huddling together of the conservatives. In response to condolences from Berlin on the death of his father, Aleksandr the Third said that "my father has fallen on the breach, but it is Christian society which was struck down with him. It is lost unless all the social forces unite to defend and save it." Russia, therefore, swallowed its pride and, with Germany and Austria, rebuilt the Alliance of the Three Emperors. Bismarck said that its aim should be to promote a "gradual partition of Turkey."

The alliance was too divided for that. Austria and Germany gained diplomatically in Turkish Europe, increasing their ties with Serbia, Romania, and Greece. Even the Bulgarians, for whom Russia had fought in 1877, were drawn more and more into the Austrian orbit. When Russia tried to pressure them, Bismarck joined with England, Austria, and Italy to restrain Russia. Bismarck ordered the Reichsbank not to accept Russian securities as collateral for loans. This amounted to driving Russia out of German financial markets. Only France gave the tsar a meager support, taking the fateful step of encouraging the French purchase of Russian securities and initiating a financial relationship. Russia nevertheless had to back down in the Balkans. Was this the time for France and Russia to link up? Bismarck wondered if there might already be a Franco-Russian alliance, in view of the agitation for it in the French press by the prominent *revanchiste* Paul Deroulède and in the Russian by the Pan-Slav Mikhail Katkov. Bismarck did his best to prevent it. He contrived a Reinsurance Treaty with Russia. But even that slender thread was cut when Bismarck was dismissed by the incoming Kaiser Wilhelm the Second in 1890.

Russian conservatism had been mollified by alliance with Bismarck's Germany and the Habsburg Empire in different combinations. But Russia and Austria were bound to clash over the spoils of receding Ottoman power in the Balkans. Bismarck had been able to manage this without isolating Russia, but the new kaiser dismissed him and almost casually dropped his German-Russian Reinsurance Treaty.

Russia turned to alliance with France and, with the aid of French and Belgian capital, embarked on its own industrial revolution. The energetic Finance Minister, Count Sergei Witte, put Russia on the gold standard and eagerly courted foreign investment in a number of projects, the grandest of which was the building of a Trans-Siberian railway. Witte thought this project "would not only bring about the opening of Siberia, but would revolutionize world trade, supersede the Suez Canal as the leading route to China, enable Russia to flood the Chinese market with textiles and metal goods, and secure political control of northern China." Thus Russia appeared in force in the Far East just as Japan and the United States were emerging as potential Far Eastern powers.

Russian leaders, along with those of the other powers, thought of China in the same way as they thought of the tottering Ottoman Empire. Jules Ferry called Manchu China the "sick man of the Far East." China's defeat at the hands of Japan in a war over Korea in 1895–1896 threw her into turmoil and nativist revolt. When the powers arrived to suppress the Boxer rebellion they exacted concessions that seemed to suggest that partition of China might be on the menu, just as partition of Turkey had seemed to be in the 1840s. Witte had already negotiated Russian control over a rail line through Manchuria (the Chinese-Eastern railway) and gained access by rail to Port Arthur in 1898. But other adventurous elements at court thought he was too soft and that Russia should have Korea as well, Japan or no Japan. Finally the tsar dropped Witte in 1903 and launched a forward policy in the Far East.

Britain would have liked to oppose Russia in Manchuria except for being bogged down in the Boer War. Failing to enlist Germany in the task of containing Russia, the British turned to Japan with whom they made an aggressive alliance in 1902. This raised the possibility of a fight with Japan over Manchuria and Korea in which the Russians would be sponsored by the French and the Japanese by the English. The Russians did not fear a local contest with Japan. On the contrary, Interior Minister Pleve, mindful of the considerable unrest in south Russia caused by a wave of strikes in 1903, was said to have expressed a certain wistful hope for a "short victorious war."

The Russo-Japanese War of 1904–1905 was, however, neither short nor victorious. With each setback suffered by Russian troops at the Far Eastern front, the revolutionary situation at home deepened. It seemed that civil society saw the war as an opening to assert itself. When the Japanese attacked Port Arthur with torpedo boats in February 1904 and their armies poured across Korea and the Liaotung peninsula, *zemstvo* liberals attempted to organize self-government to aid the war effort. In July, Pleve himself was assassinated by a terrorist. The fall of Port Arthur in January 1905 was followed by "Bloody Sunday," the government's attack, with over a thousand casualties, on a peaceful workers' demonstration led by a priest, Father Gapon. The demonstrators had been told by Gapon that God would protect them and that the tsar, the "Little Father," would hear their pleas. But these were answered by the rattle of machine-gun fire. That was the last time the Russian workers ever marched behind icons and pictures of the tsar. Mukden fell in March 1905, and the navy was defeated at Tsushima in May. In June there occurred the mutiny on the battleship *Potemkin*, later fabled in Sergei Eisenstein's film of the same name, and a broad outbreak of peasant rebellion.

The war was ended by the Peace of Portsmouth, September 1905, according to which Japan got Korea, a leasehold on the Liaotung peninsula, and south Sakhalin island. Count Witte, who had been called back to sign the peace, won for his pains the nickname of "Count Half-Sakhalin" (*Graf polovina Sakhalina*). The end of war did not, however, end the revolution at home. European Russia was in effect still denuded of troops. The rail workers staged a strike that quickly turned into a general strike. The two capitals were cut off from each other. Moreover, the strike committee decided that it should become a workers' council, a *soviet*, arrogating to itself a kind of semi-governmental authority. Lev Davidovien Bronstein (Trotsky) was to be elected as its president. In defense Tsar Nicholas the Second offered his October Manifesto, promising a constitution with a Duma, a strengthened Council of Ministers, and Count Witte as the first prime minister. An influential wing of liberals split from the revolutionary movement to accept the tsar's offer, taking the name Octobrists. Over the next two years some concessions were taken back as the troops returned and the French contributed a massive loan that freed the tsar from reliance on the Duma. Pëtr Stolypin, Prime Minister from 1906 to 1911, suppressed the revolution by means of a protracted campaign, which featured widespread executions (the hangman's noose earned the term "Stolypin necktie") and a kind of semi-official encouragement of the paramilitary "Black Hundreds," in whom some historians have seen a hint of a proto-fascism. He also successfully prevented the radical majorities of the first two Dumas from carrying out a drastic land reform.

But much of what had transpired in 1905 could not be eradicated. The throne had managed to foil the movement for a democratic republic, but it was no longer an integrated autocracy. The country's various social forces now called themselves political parties in the

Western sense. There were two liberal parties. The Constitutional Democrats (Kadets) represented the combined forces of the Union of Unions (a central organization of mostly white-collar unions), the zemstvo constitutionalists, progressive industrialists, and Legal Marxists. The Kadet program was universal suffrage, land reform with compensation, a progressive income tax, workers' health insurance, and factory inspection. Its left wing was led by the distinguished historian Pavel Miliukov and the ex–Legal Marxist Pëtr Struve. On the right was V. A. Maklakov, who feared the revolution and regarded the Kadets' radical democratic stance as an error, thinking instead that its natural allies were progressive civil servants who might move the tsar to reform from above.

Maklakov would have preferred the Kadets to be more like the Octobrists (who had accepted the Tsar's offer of a constitution in his October Manifesto). The latter were a party of industrialists, liberal landlords, and civil servants. Octobrists aimed mostly to resist land reform and urged a restricted suffrage and indirect elections. The industrialists who filled their ranks had flirted with the idea of opposition as long as the tsar persisted in seeing them as a menace to the social order. At the turn of the century, when the bizarre experiment with a police trade unionism under S. V. Zubatov was essayed, police agents led strikes for economic and political demands. Zubatov had sold the Interior Ministry on the notion of workers providing a check on the ambitions of progressive factory owners, Jews ("the crudity of the Jew-bosses"), and other disloyal elements. Father Gapon had risen in the labor movement originally as a Zubatovist. But the movement had to be disbanded after a series of strikes that it stirred up in south Russia in 1903 caused the government to fear it more than the liberal factory owners. With Zubatovism a dead letter, industrialists could adopt a more friendly position on the monarchy. Perhaps this relationship was abetted by the generous monopoly pricing agreements that protected cartels in the iron and steel, rails, coal, and other industries. Industry thus enjoyed a kind of *zaibatsu* status in a corporate state. In view of the highly statist nature of this Russian economic policy, it was easy for industrialists to suppose that their situation was comparable to that of the German industrialists who enjoyed the benefits of state paternalism and friendly relations with the agrarians in a "marriage of iron and rye." When German Chancellor Bulow called Germany "a well-tended garden," he was describing an ideal much admired in Russia as well.

In addition to the liberal parties, there was a wide assortment of lesser parties led by monarchists and nationalists. But the Socialist

Revolutionary party (SRs) had the greatest potential, uniting as it did the intelligentsia tradition of the nineteenth-century *narodnichestvo* and a peasant constituency that was bound to dwarf the other parties electorally for generations to come. The SRs stood by the slogan of the Black Repartition faction of Populist militants of the 1870s from whose ranks Plekhanov had come. That is, they embodied a collectivist agrarian idea that could only come into fruition as the result of a revolutionary upheaval sweeping the whole country. It could hardly be said that they had any economic policy beyond this. As a ruling party they would certainly have had political chances comparable to the agrarian parties that ruled for a time in Poland, Bulgaria, and some other East European states in the 1920s. But they would have been prone to the same social and economic crises and might perhaps have been pushed aside by the same sort of authoritarian forces of the right.

The industrial workers were spoken for by the wildly fissiparous Russian Social Democracy, its militants all owing allegiance to the Second International of socialist parties and the German Social Democracy in particular. The main center had split before the revolution into Bolsheviks (men of the majority) and Mensheviks (men of the minority) according to a tangled series of maneuvers at the second congress of the Social Democracy in 1903. Their differences in matters of program at that time were insignificant. They had split because of "the organization question." Vladimir Ulianov (Lenin) and the Bolsheviks held that a secret and highly professional apparatus was essential for work under conditions of illegality inside Russia. Iulii Martov and the Mensheviks found dangers in this "Jacobin" organizational ideal that called up memories of the Populist Peoples' Will who had assassinated Aleksandr the Second. They called Bolshevism a kind of Carbonarism, referring to the *carbonari* (charcoal burners) of the early nineteenth century, secret societies who swore blood oaths and performed other lurid rituals. Thus Mensheviks tried to denounce the Bolsheviks to the German Social Democrats as a throwback and an embarrassment to the international movement. The Germans, however, refused to intervene on a purely organizational matter that did not touch program and tactics to grant Menshevism the Russian franchise. There remained two competing factions of the same party until 1912.

The Mensheviks drew from the experience of the revolution of 1905 the lesson that they should not play any role in a coming revolution more ambitious than to form the nucleus of a labor opposition, a "loyal opposition" on the British model. They should stay out of any revolutionary government, since it could only be the agent of a bourgeois revolution. Nevertheless, in 1917 the war would cause them to ignore all this and join a Provisional Government that certainly was not an agent of socialist transformation.

On the other side, the Bolsheviks in June 1905 had put forward the slogan of a Revolutionary Democratic Dictatorship of the Proletariat and the Peasantry. This was not a socialist slogan; a democratic dictatorship would make no inroads on private property. It was merely an incantation of the democratic dictatorship of the Jacobins of 1793. The Jacobinism that Martov had divined in Lenin's organization model was now made flesh in the political program under whose banner the Bolsheviks would march up to April 1917. This suggested readiness to join with all representatives of the broad democracy who wanted to secure political freedom, even, said Lenin, "Messrs. Marshals of the Nobility" (an ephemeral liberal gentry party). But the Bolsheviks would not be part of any such multi-party government in 1917.

None of the Russian social democrats could conjecture, on the basis of theory or experience, a future revolutionary government that would break with the norms of a democratic republic. Lenin's description of the aims of the democratic movement demonstrates this. And none of them could envision the future revolution resulting in a socialist state. Or almost none: Only the maverick Trotsky, who had been the president of the Saint Petersburg Soviet in October 1905, suggested a prognosis based on his 1905 experience. The Soviet had been a purely proletarian institution; moreover, it had acted with definite semi-governmental pretension. Suppose then that the Soviet was the germ of a socialist dictatorship of the proletariat? This might be a pipedream, but it might also be forced on the social democrats by a repeat of October 1905. If a general strike, a movement for an eight-hour day, or some other manifestation were put forward by the workers through the Soviet, it would undoubtedly be answered by the employers declaring lockouts. The revolutionary state, even Lenin's Democratic Dictatorship, would be forced to a choice: break the strike and end the revolution or nationalize the factories in question and start on the path to socialism. The workers themselves, casting aside the spirit of self-abnegation required by Lenin's prognoses, would force the social democracy into this choice. To decide for the workers would mean embarking on the way of "permanent revolution," a process that begins with democracy but ultimately solves the problem of democracy by means of socialism.

Trotsky was a Menshevik who had arrived at a vision of the future that other Mensheviks could never accept. He was also a most biting critic of Lenin's Jacobinism in organization and in program. He alone among social democrats peered into the future and saw a socialist Russia. But there were many active anarchists who, having no Marxism to guide them, believed that anything was possible, even a collectivist Russia. If the country were again to collapse in revolution, the anarchists would have a chance to set the tone.

The years between the revolution and the world war are usually considered a time of semi-constitutional experiment. The Duma started out looking like a radical Long Parliament. The first elections gave it a Kadet majority, an artificial one in view of the fact that the SRs and Social Democrats boycotted it. The country was gripped by counterrevolutionary violence with hangings and pogroms. The Duma voted no confidence in the government and was quickly dissolved, after which the liberal deputies issued the Vyborg Manifesto, calling on the people to refuse taxes or conscription until a new Duma was elected. This was a kind of high-water mark for liberalism in its radical and revolutionary clothing, which it was subsequently to discard.

The second Duma was more representative and showed signs of voting a sweeping land reform before Stolypin dissolved it. He thereupon promulgated a new electoral law designed to get conservative majorities. It was calculated that an elector might gain office through the votes of 230 landowners, 1,000 bourgeois, 15,000 lower middle class, 60,000 peasants, or 125,000 workers. Stolypin's coup produced an Octobrist and right majority for the next two Dumas, which sat up to the outbreak of revolution in 1917. It passed further laws on pacification. Stolypin also pushed through a wide-ranging land reform intended to wreck the peasant commune. He ended commune responsibility for taxes and divided land taken from the communes among millions of peasants. His "wager on the strong and sober" was designed to destroy the commune as a presumed center of the plans of radicals and to create on the countryside a class of smallholders loyal to the regime. No gentry land, as a rule the best land, was touched. The same for crown-owned forests and meadows. The Stolypin reforms succeeded in separating from the communes around 10 percent of their lands and about the same proportion of peasants. There were around six million landowning peasants in 1914. That did not stop the peasants from voting for a party called the Socialist Revolutionaries, nor from staging a peasant war in 1917, one in which the communes were centers of agitation for seizure of the landlords' lands. Back in 1899, Lenin had concluded an exhaustive economic work on the Russian internal market with the thought that the future must decide on two possible solutions to the agrarian question: an "American" one put in place by a "black repartition" of the land and the establishment of a vast yeoman class of individual proprietors, or a "Prussian" solution in which the biggest landlords maintained their hold on a modernizing country. To use his terms, Russia had chosen for a Prussian solution.

Stolypin did not know how to tackle the problems of the urban working class, but they almost seemed to go away. Strikes at any rate were fewer and fewer up to the time of his mysterious assassination in 1911. Then, beginning with a strike in the Lena gold fields that ended in a massacre, strikes increased dramatically, reaching by 1914 the same level as in 1905. On the eve of the war, those in the tsar's government who made the fateful decisions had to do so under the threat of vast urban industrial strife and violence. Nevertheless one cannot say that the tsarist economic policy had failed in its aims. The economy continued to grow right up to the war, with a stable currency. Foreign investment by that time amounted to probably one third of the total; of that perhaps a third was French, centered in textiles and southern metallurgy. British capital was concentrated in the oil of the Caucasus, with German in Polish textiles, copper mining, and electronics. Just under half of the banking capital in the country was foreign owned.

Was Russia solving its problems prior to the outbreak of war? Soviet historians used to insist that it was not and could not. Western writers thought the opposite: that only the war plunged Russia into chaos and ruin. In the 1980s it became more common for Western historians to argue that the problems of Russian society were pointing her toward revolution, war or no war. But, since the fall of the Soviet power in 1991, Russian writers have been again arguing that the Duma years were a time of opportunities lost. So the pendulum continues to swing. It is difficult to imagine the country turning to revolution and Bolshevik dictatorship outside the context of war. Yet even in peace the Russia that survived would have had internal problems at least as great as those of Imperial Germany owing to its lack of political modernization alongside its continuing agrarian problem and general backwardness. Maintaining an old regime that was modernizing industrially without recourse to dictatorship of the right might have proved difficult. And it also has to be asked whether a conservative yet industrially robust Russia with a forward foreign policy could have worked out its differences with the other powers in the contentious era of imperial expansion.

CHAPTER 4

The Empire Goes to War

As long as the tsar pursued adventure in the Far East, he had been encouraged by his cousin the kaiser who braced him to stand up for the white man against the Yellow Peril. The tsar was certainly less likely while so engaged to raise objections to German plans for a Berlin-to-Baghdad railway across Russia's southern periphery. However, Russian defeat at the hands of Japan changed everything. As would again be demonstrated just a dozen years later, defeat meant revolution. All over Asia news of the Russian events was a caress to the ear of anyone who sought the overthrow of Western imperialism. Asian nationalists took the defeat of Russia by non-Europeans as a boon and the Russian revolution as a signal of triumphs to come. Sun Yat-sen called Russia the most tyrannical regime on earth and hailed the movement to overthrow it. Like others who saw things this way, Sun was more excited about the constitutional and democratic hopes awakened by the revolution than by its proletarian leadership.

This was also the sense of the bazaar and the mullahs in Persia who rose up against the Qajar dynasty Shah Muzaffar ed-Din in 1906, protected up to then by Russian Cossack troops. Like the liberals in Russia, the Persian revolutionaries saw the chance to come abreast of British constitutional political culture and fully expected their moves to be greeted with approval in England. The mullahs were especially impressed to see Muslims sitting as a confessional party in the first Russian Duma. On the other side, the counterrevolution in Russia set it as an urgent task to defeat the Persian rebellion as soon as its own was under control.

The Russian events also thrilled Western radicals. They saw in the general strike of October 1905 an indication of the proletariat in action. A generation of Western Social Democrats had become accustomed to the idea that theirs was a peaceful, legal, parliamentary movement that had long since passed the time when it would depend on strikes and direct action by the working class. Those who did call for strikes were usually syndicalists (from the French *syndicat*, trade union) or anarchists. In the German Social Democracy, however, it was said that "the general strike is general nonsense." Russia seemed to have changed all that. Rosa Luxemburg, a leftist German and Polish Social Democrat, welcomed the new worker militancy and urged that the social Democracy adopt the general strike as a vehicle for political action. This was not far from Trotsky's idea of the "permanent revolution" in Russia. The ideological divide between the Social Democracy and anarchism, once so absolute and binding, was being bridged by Social Democrats advocating tactics of direct action that had been left to anarchists and anarcho-syndicalists for a generation.

Defeat and revolution also had the effect of making Russia more eligible for the friendship of Britain. At the time of the British alliance with Japan in 1902, it was immediately realized that a Russo-Japanese war might pit Britain, as the ally of Japan, against France, the ally of Russia. To localize the conflict and prevent this, the British and the French made an entente in 1904. Along with its far-reaching global compromises, the entente promised to France that Britain would look with favor on a future French annexation of Morocco. In effect, Morocco was compensation to France for the entente. The Germans, however, launched a demand for compensation of their own, perhaps in Africa or somewhere else. This was refused by the British and the French.

The Moroccan crisis was a byproduct of the Russo-Japanese War in the Far East. On Morocco, Germany was faced with a coalition of opponents. The Kaiser tried to pull Russia into the Western dispute by a pact signed at a secret meeting between him and his cousin the Tsar, their two yachts dropping anchor at Björkö on the Finnish coast in the summer of 1905. The two met without their staffs. The Kaiser called it "a fine lark." He cited the primacy of the monarchical principle. The Tsar wanted diplomatic help in the Far East and hoped to break up the Anglo-Japanese alliance. But the French, who were paying the bills for Russia, now a Russia fighting to restore order after a revolution, would have none of it. Björkö was a dead letter. Instead, Russia dutifully lined up on the side of the French at the conference of Algeciras, which finally settled the Moroccan crisis.

But Björkö had already made a strong impression on Britain. It would have been in effect a merger of the Franco-Russian alliance and the Triple alliance, which would have amounted to a continental league against Britain. A new urgency arose in the British attitude toward Russia. This was coupled with growing British unease about Germany, in gestation as far back as the German expressions of sympathy for the Boers in 1895 and the German navy bills at the turn of the century. The British decided that having Russia at the Straits was not so bad after all. As long as the Russians could be prevented from resuming their march toward India in Central Asia, Britain could make a colonial entente with them in the same spirit as the Anglo-French entente of 1904.

This the two powers did in 1907. They called off a potential quarrel over Tibet by recognizing Chinese supremacy there. They recognized British power over Afghanistan. They made common cause in the suppression of the Persian revolution, much to the disappointment of the Persian revolutionaries who thought that they were in ideological harmony with Britain. The Anglo-Russian entente divided Persia into three zones, Britain ascendant in the south and Russia in the north. Britain and Russia, the two main contestants of the nineteenth century in the Great Game for control of Asia, whose conflicts had more or less defined world politics since Napoleon, who had fought over the Near Eastern Question in Crimea and the crises of the 1870s and 1880s, finally came to terms.

The Anglo-Russian entente brightened prospects for the British in what would later be called the Middle East. Russia might also be a potential British supporter against Germany on the Baghdad railway. Did the entente mean as well British encouragement for Russia at the Straits? That was strongly indicated by the English King Edward the Seventh's meeting with Tsar Nicholas at Reval (Tallinn) in June 1908. The "Reval interview" seemed to be a green light for Russian action. This was at any rate the way it was perceived by the Ottoman officers known as the Young Turks who took power over the Empire in July. Their revolution was inspired by the Russian movement of 1905 and its brief imitation in Iran. They wanted to stave off the pending partition of the empire by an effort at constitutional reform and a more conciliatory policy toward the subject nationalities.

This occurred at the time when a new doctrine, Neo-Slavism, was winning adherents among Russian liberals. Pëtr Struve and Prince Trubetskoy argued that Russia must forget about Asia for the moment and turn to the Balkans and the Black Sea to build her power there in a quiet way that would be amenable to the Western powers. The Straits question, they thought, would solve itself over time. Neo-Slavism did not repeat the old Pan-Slav appeal for the unity of the Slavs under the Tsar but called instead for a federation of constitutional Slavic states, Catholic or Orthodox, a federation that might even include the Ukraine and Poland. Both Pan-Slavism and Neo-Slavism focused attention on Austria-Hungary and a looming competition for the affection of the Balkan Slavs. When the Young Turks made their revolution in 1908, they had in mind something similar for the Slavs in the Ottoman Empire. Like the Neo-Slavs in Russia they embraced attitudes that would later be described as Wilsonian. They all looked to the British or, more specifically, to the Anglo-French entente.

Russian Foreign Minister A. P. Izvolsky saw new possibilities in a policy that did not threaten the West in the Far East or in Central Asia. He wanted to take advantage of the new perspectives offered by a presumably weaker and more pliant Turkey. Earlier in the year Austria had floated a project for a railway through the Sanjak of Novi Pazar and farther through Macedonia to Salonika, thus dividing Serbia and Montenegro. Izvolsky had successfully opposed this. But after the Young Turk revolution he offered Austrian foreign minister Aehrenthal a chance to annex Bosnia (nominally Ottoman but occupied by Austria since 1878). In return Russia was to have control over the Straits, that is, use of them by Russian warships coupled with denial of their use to others. Izvolsky thought he had made a brilliant bargain. But he could not get it approved in Paris and London, and while he was trying to do so, Austria preemptively annexed Bosnia.

Izvolsky thought he had been had. So did Serbia, who had long had earmarks on Bosnia. In March 1909, the angry Serbs mobilized a little army to attack Bosnia with Russian encouragement. But Germany came down hard on both Serbia and Russia, demanding that Izvolsky restrain Serbia—and more than that, publicly agree to accept the Austrian annexation of Bosnia. Izvolsky had to back down and make Serbia back down as well. Kiderlen-Wachter, the head of the German foreign office, boasted that to make Russia back down, it had been necessary to "thump the table." Austria-Hungary would probably have gone to war with Serbia if the Russians had not been frightened off. The conclusion drawn in Saint Petersburg was that, if humiliations on this order were not to become a steady diet in the future, it would be necessary to overhaul and prepare the armed forces from top to bottom. In Belgrade it was similarly resolved to give greater support to Yugo-Slav propaganda and terrorists operating within Austrian lines.

In 1910 Izvolsky yielded the Foreign Ministry to S. D. Sazonov and went as Ambassador to Paris. Russia encouraged Italy to move against the Turks in Tripolitania while it tried again in 1911 to get Turkey to yield on the Straits. But the Turks did not bite. When the Italian forces succeeded in tying down large numbers of Turkish troops in North Africa, the Russians used the opportunity to promote a Balkan League—Serbia, Montenegro, Bulgaria, and Greece—and its preparations for war against Turkey to redraw the map of the Balkans. Every small Balkan state was eager to gain new territories by force.

The Balkan War of 1912 saw them all successful against the Turks. The Bulgarians pressed into Macedonia and West Thrace, the Greeks into Salonika, and the Serbs into the Sanjak and up to the Albanian coast. "They brought their steeds to water in the Adriatic," said an admiring King Nicholas of Montenegro. Austria now announced that it would not tolerate Serbian expansion to the Adriatic and came out for an independent Albania. The Austrians mobilized troops to threaten Serbia. In turn, Russia mobilized troops in the Caucasus to threaten Turkey. But at the last minute Russia again backed down. It was a repeat of the Russian humiliation of 1908–1909.

Peace was made and the new Balkan powers pocketed their gains. A second Balkan war was fought in 1913 largely to re-divide Macedonia and make some other changes. The Albanian problem, however, continued to fester, with Serbia conducting periodic raids into the territory of the new state. Austria warned and warned. The Kaiser even expressed readiness for war with Serbia, telling the Austrians, "I stand by you and am ready to draw the saber whenever your action makes it necessary." Ready to draw the saber against Russia, to support Albania! On his side, Sazonov told the Serbs to leave Albania alone and to be content for the moment with her other gains, to be ready "when the time comes to lance the Austro-Hungarian abscess, which has not come to a head as has the Turkish one." Ready to liquidate two vast multinational empires!

On the eve of the War, a Russian official, P. N. Durnovo, a former Minister of the Interior and member of the State Council, issued a prescient warning about the future. He was especially impressed by the disadvantage of Russia's entente with Britain and the catastrophic consequences should it bring Russia into war with Germany. There were no real conflicts of interest between Russia and Germany, he argued, and both upheld the principle of monarchy in a hostile world. On the other hand, the contest between England and Germany was the core of current world politics. But they were not vulnerable to each other. Nothing the British could do to Germany in war would defeat her. The main burden of fighting Germany, therefore, would fall on Russia, contending with the best armies in the world, facing with all her deficiencies in rail transport and other areas, the threat of costly attrition and military defeat. As a result of this defeat, Durnovo warned, "Russia will be flung into hopeless anarchy, the issue of which will be hard to foresee."

Matters would all come to a head a year later after an odd interlude of feverish war preparations among the great powers mixed with earnest and anguished peace efforts. Everyone expected war and faced the prospect without panic. The Archduke Franz Ferdinand visited Sarajevo on the anniversary of the battle of Kosovo of 1389. He was an advocate of Trialism, a plan for south Slav autonomy in the Habsburg Empire. Serbian nationalist terrorists saw the menace in this and managed to kill him and his wife. When the Austrian court heard the news it was livid and resolved to "crush Serbia." In the name of the defense of the monarchic principle the Germans supported the local war against Serbia. It was finally the Russians who broadened the conflict by coming to Serbia's aid. They had backed down in 1908 and in 1912, but not this time. Russia mobilized her forces against Austria-Hungary and Germany, throwing her power into the crisis that would result in the world war.

War quickly enveloped everything in its grip. The European Socialist parties with only a few exceptions voted to defend their countries and in most cases to join war governments. The German Socialists cited the need to stop the reactionary tsardom that appears in the writings of Marx. The French invoked the traditions of Jacobinism and the Paris Commune. Patriotic appeals came from prominent older anarchists such as Jean Grave, the "Pope of European anarchism." The small bloc of left deputies to the last Duma, elected under the restrictive laws of 1907, five Bolsheviks, six Mensheviks, and 10 from the Trudovik party of Aleksandr Kerensky, refused to vote war credits and then walked out. But Plekhanov broke with Menshevik "Internationalism" and joined the dean of the anarchists Pëtr Kropotkin in urging support for Russia on the grounds that it defended France, "the foyer of free thought, the land of the great revolution." The mobilization took place and the fighting proceeded into the following year before any major international protest could be launched.

Antiwar Socialists finally met at Zimmerwald in Switzerland in 1915. The Zimmerwaldists voted a historic resolution calling for "a peace without annexations or indemnities" and a redrawing of the future map of Europe according to the idea of "national self-determination." These phrases were to ring in the ears of the world for the next generation. Lenin, however, thought they were all nonsense and that Zimmerwald was "a muckheap." He wanted instead a clear break with the "social patriotism" of the Socialist parties, the proclamation of a new international, and, most importantly, the transformation of the war into a civil war. Appeals to peace would not avail, he said; the governments would only relent when their armies fell apart in revolution. Lenin, who had earlier written during the Russo-Japanese War of "the advantages of having one's country defeated in war," now began to see with insight that defeat in itself would be the revolution for which he had waited all his life. Trotsky, who had drafted the Zimmerwald Manifesto, spoke in a similar vein but also occasionally expressed fears that the defeat of France would mean the triumph of "the feudal-monarchical" idea over the "democratic-republican" one. He averred, however, that real socialists wanted revolution so badly that they would countenance defeat to achieve it. Lenin's position was slightly different: defeat is itself revolution; socialists must urge defeat, value defeat, press for defeat, love defeat.

Lenin was soon to publish an essay on imperialism laying a theoretical foundation for these aims. It argued from a welter of statistics that big banks had arisen everywhere and big firms alongside them, along with imperialist foreign policies. His conclusion was that the economic facts had caused this. The world should now consider itself to be in the phase of capitalism henceforth to be known as Imperialism. This was no theoretical tour de force, even for those who had not read Rosa Luxemburg, Rudolf Hilferding, or Otto Bauer on the subject. But the real point was to put a theoretical foundation beneath the idea that, in the era of Imperialism, Marxists could no longer behave as Marx and Engels had done; they could no longer base action on war according to a judgment of which outcome would best benefit the working class as a whole. In the era of Imperialism, defeatism was the only policy for a revolutionary. In 1916 Lenin despaired of ever seeing this revolution in his lifetime. But he need not have, for defeat was right around the corner.

CHAPTER 5

1917

Russia's society and polity buckled under the strain of a long war. But no country was prepared for a war of such scale. The horrors of the combat that we know best from films such as Lewis Milestone's *All Quiet on the Western Front* and Stanley Kubrick's *Paths of Glory*, or from the war poetry of Wilfred Owen and Siegfried Sassoon, were for the ordinary soldier most concentrated and nightmarish on the western front. This was because the tremendous advantage of the defense was most accentuated where the front was the narrowest. In the east, however, there was the same fortification of positions by machine guns and wire, the same fiendishly accurate registration of artillery, the same mud and gore, but a wider front and a good deal more room to maneuver. As a result, where the battles in the west were often fought over hundreds of yards of terrain, in the east there were more numerous penetrations. A seeming breakthrough might be made for the moment and a large salient might bulge into the enemy's territory. Nevertheless, counterattacks against the flanks of the salient would inevitably follow; it would be reduced, and finally eliminated. Counting up the losses, one would find that hundreds of thousands had been lost for nothing. So it was, or nearly so, with the Brusilov offensive of 1916, which, while it broke the offensive capacity of the Austrian army for the rest of the war, gained only about 20 miles north of Lemberg at a cost of half a million men. General Brusilov, who would later end up with a command in the Red Army, boasted that this was nothing compared to what the Russian armies would be able to accomplish in another year.

Russia had mobilized over 15 million men. Organizing and equipping them for combat would have meant reshaping the entire society as a new Sparta. Coordination of the vast tasks of the war effort entrenched the state in every phase of Russian life, in a kind of rickety imitation of the regime that Generals Ludendorff and Hindenburg were running in Germany. As Ludendorff would later explain, this was the first model for "totalitarian war." In Russia, it did not require the suppression of the semi-parliamentary system that had been worked out by the Stolypin coup of 1907. The nation seemed to sense the need for defense of the Russian earth as it was described in war propaganda. As in 1905 this even gave some room for initiative to the liberals in their work of organizing support for the war. Once again they sought to use the war as a rationale to advance claims for the broadening of local self-government. The two liberal parties, the Kadets and Octobrists, were the core of the Progressive Bloc that kept the Duma pliant.

Yet the task was too great. Industry failed to replace the arms and the shells consumed at a rate no one could have foreseen. Many of the most-skilled workers were sent to the front and perished among the first of the fallen. Their places at the bench were taken by peasants, often by women and children. The railroads proved incapable of supplying the long front. Internal logistics were complicated by the fact that the Turks had kept Russia's navy out of the Black Sea and the threat of German minefields kept the British fleet out of the Baltic, so supplies had to come in from Murmansk and Vladivostok. Those that arrived could not always get to where they were needed. In Central Asia mobilization provoked a violent resistance. When Kazakh and Kirghiz men were drafted for noncombatant duty in 1916 they rebelled and had to be suppressed with troops. Hundreds of thousands of local citizens who supported the revolt were driven from their lands. But there was no hesitation about using force to maintain discipline. In the summer after the Brusilov offensive, anti-war strikes and bread riots began to break out in Moscow and other Russian towns.

The state tried to tighten things up. Tsar Nicholas took over personal command of the general staff, to the encouragement of the Tsarina Aleksandra, the former Princess Alix of Hesse. "You have never lost an opportunity to show your love and kindness," she wrote to him, "now let them feel your fist! They themselves ask for this. So many have recently said to me: 'We need the whip!' This is strange, but such is the Slavic nature—the greatest firmness, even cruelty and at the same time—warm love. They must learn to fear you. Love is not enough."

The Tsar was greatly bolstered by the Tsarina, and she by Rasputin, "the dissolute one," a itinerant holy man from the order of the *khlysty*, an outlawed sect given to orgies and other enthusiasms. He was married, with four children. He had bounced around Palestine and Greece and had been kept for a time among the gaggle of faith healers at the Montenegrin court. He ended up in Saint Petersburg in 1907 and freely supplied advice to the crown about a range of issues. Not all of it was bad. He warned, for example, against Russia's involvement, or further involvement, in the Balkan wars. The Tsarina valued his apparent ability to heal the young Tsarevich Aleksei's attacks of hemophilia. He had a wide circle of prominent female admirers and the reputation of a party animal. More important, he was said to have had some influence on the numerous changes in the government, a "ministerial leapfrog," as some Duma wits called it, involving four Prime Ministers, six Interior Ministers, three Foreign Ministers, four War Ministers, and even four Procurators of the Holy Synod. Some of these had German names. That was no mystery. Baltic German barons had figured prominently in the Russian army and civil service since the time of Peter the Great. Nevertheless, when the reputedly dim Boris Stürmer, a politician who had risen through his connections to Rasputin's circle, became Premier in January 1916, Paul Miliukov, speaking for the Progressive Bloc, launched a vehement protest that ended with the words: "Is this stupidity or treason?"

The press wrapped up all the problems the regime was facing into a neat bundle and called them the fault of the Germans at court, the "German woman," and especially of Rasputin. This gave rise to the idea that a coup removing Rasputin might set things aright. In December 1916, Aleksandr Guchkov, the leader of the Octobrists, and Prince Yusupov, in pursuit of this thought, lured Rasputin to a "party" at which they laboriously assassinated him. In killing Rasputin, however, they also killed the myth that things had gone wrong only because of him. In fact, nothing changed. Fears of a new 1905 mounted. What would the state have against the outbreak of another general strike in the capital? Perhaps the 160,000 troops around the city and the 12,000 in the guard units in the garrison. In the event of a general strike these would be pitted against the high concentration of workers in the war industries, swollen to around 400,000. All of the individuals on both sides were to be actors in the great drama that was unfolding.

The overthrow of the Tsar occurred at the end of February 1917. The food situation was desperate, with large queues for bread. A big march for International Women's Day (March 8 according to the Western calendar, February 23 according to the Julian calendar in use until the Bolsheviks came to power) was followed by some strikes at factories employing mostly women. There had been strikes among the "match girls" employed in match factories. On the day after the march, a strike broke out at the Putilov metal works and developed into a general strike of some 200,000 workers by February 25. This was Rosa Luxemburg's idea of the mass strike brought to life. The city turned into a vast demonstration, with seemingly spontaneous attacks on the police coupled with fraternization with the soldiers. Force had to be used against it. On February 25 the firing on the crowds began. That night the Volinsky regiment, one of the units that had dispersed a crowd with machine guns, held a meeting to decide whether they would do it again. One of its officers, Captain Lashevich, gave a rousing speech in favor of following orders and defending the regime. He lost the vote and was shot on the spot. Having taking such a step the mutineers could not turn back. They marched on the other units to urge them to follow suit, with the result that the troops quickly joined them in refusing orders to fire. The garrison in effect melted away. The monarchy was finished.

On February 26 the Tsar dissolved the Duma, and a council of elders appointed some members of the Progressive Bloc as the Provisional Committee of the Duma. But alongside the Provisional Committee there was formed an Executive Committee of the Petrograd Soviet of Workers and Soldiers Deputies—not merely a Soviet of Workers Deputies as in 1905, but now a Soviet of Workers *and Soldiers* Deputies. Once again the inherent semi-governmental pretensions of a workers' council appeared. This situation, a repetition of 1905, has been called the Dual Power. The Soviet immediately issued the famous Order Number One: arrest the tsarist ministers; occupy the banks, the mint, the printing offices; send from the units of the garrison one deputy for every 1,000 soldiers. The Soviet was on the way to the overthrow of the tsar by arresting his ministers; the next step would have been to proclaim a republic. On the other side, the Provisional Committee sought to derail these plans by finding a successor to Tsar Nicholas, perhaps the grand Duke Mikhail as Regent to the Tsarevich. But these plans did not take hold. The Tsar had to abdicate in favor of a Provisional Government to be led by representatives of the Octobrists and Kadets. Its name gave an idea of the modesty of its authority. The real power could only be constituted, everyone agreed, by elections for a Constituent Assembly. But no date was given for that. In fact, it made sense to fear an election, as it could only be a referendum on the war.

How did the people feel about all this? In the absence of polls, we have no way of gauging public opinion such as would have been reflected in a secret ballot election. But we can draw some conclusions about what might be called active public opinion from some large meetings and conventions of popular constituencies in the spring and summer. An All-Russian Congress of Peasants met May 17–June 2, with an SR delegation of 535, a nonparty delegation of 465, and 103 Social Democrats. The SRs called for a vote *against* a Bolshevik resolution, "All Land to the Peasants." The Bolsheviks had stolen the SR land program. This must have made an impression on the nonparty delegates, a bloc of votes almost as large as that of the SRs. One imagines old Ivan, the village letter writer, returning from the Congress to give a report to those who delegated him to attend. He explains to the astounded villagers that the Socialist Revolutionaries, the party of the peasantry, the repository of the tradition of *narodnichestvo*, are against the peasants taking the landlords' land in view, they say, of the pressing needs of the war effort. He continues that another party, however, the "men of the majority" (the Bolsheviks), regards the war as imperialist and advocates that the peasants seize the land. One imagines this scene played out by 465 delegates in various regions of the country.

A Petrograd Conference of Factory and Shop Committees met on May 30–June 1, with anarchists and Bolsheviks predominant. These committees had around two and a half million workers. They had seized the eight-hour day by quitting after eight hours; they had staged desperate strikes for higher wages, spurred on as they were by the sevenfold inflation of the currency since the start of the war. The anarchist delegates were influenced by the idea that all over Europe the trade unions had turned out to be nests of social patriots and slaves of parliamentarism. This was true, they thought, of both anarcho-syndicalists, who traced their doctrine from Bakunin, and anarchist communists, who traced theirs from Kropotkin, the "anarchist Prince." These were not contending schools in anarchist doctrine so much as a succession with a difference in emphasis. Bakunin put great stress on class struggle and trade unions. After his death in 1876, Kropotkin looked more to affinity groups and the promise of an immediate establishment of Communism with distribution according to need. Kropotkin and French anarchist Jean Grave, "the Pope of anarchism," had urged support for the war effort, in the name of the defense of France, "the foyer of free thought, the land of the great revolution." Revolt against the war for the younger anarchists was thus also revolt against the older anarchist ideas. Instead of the trade unions, they looked to the factory committees; instead of parliaments they looked to the soviets. An axis of factory committees and soviets might serve as a point of departure for a synthesis of the Bakunin and Kropotkin traditions, that is, for an immediate leap into stateless Communism. This was the argument of G. P. Maksimov, who split with the main body of the Petrograd anarchists then publishing *Golos Truda* (Voice of Labor), and agitated for an anarchist "synthesis" in a new organ, *Vol'nyi Golos Truda* (Free Voice of Labor). The soviets and factory committees, taken together, would become "production and consumption communes." Maksimov urged the slogan, "All Power to the Soviets and Factory Committees!"

By this time, as we shall see, Lenin and the Bolsheviks were arguing for "the Commune" and for workers' control of production. Was this the same as the anarchists' slogan? In fact, in the Bolshevik factory propaganda, Lenin's idea of workers' control meant nothing more than accounting. Throw open the books, force the employers to reveal their secrets, observe and oversee the enterprises. For the anarchists it usually meant seizure of the factory and organizing production in concert with other seized factories. Lenin and Maksimov could have engaged in a fascinating theoretical dispute about these differences. On the other hand, permitting this little misunderstanding to go uncorrected made it possible for the Bolsheviks to recruit the anarchists as their infantry. Unity was urged according to the slogan "March Separately and Strike Together." At the Conference, Bolsheviks and anarchists in a bloc voted down a Marxist-sounding Menshevik resolution for state control of industry and approved a Bolshevik-anarchist one for "workers' control." The anarchists marveled at the way that Bolshevism had broken with the old parliamentary and statist Marxism and even become anarchist.

The Bolsheviks did not make much immediate headway with other organizations. An All-Russian Congress of Soviets, meeting on June 3, had 285 SR deputies, 248 Menshevik, 105 Bolshevik. It elected a Menshevik-SR (at this point in alliance, as we shall see) executive committee that was to sit until the October revolution. An All-Russian Congress of Trade Unions, meeting June 20–28, had a Menshevik-SR majority. Here the mood was opposite that in the factory committees. The Congress passed a Menshevik resolution on state control of industry. The Bolsheviks were never to win the trade unions. They knew they could only succeed by advancing the old Populist slogan of the "black repartition" and in winning the anarchist workers with their advocacy of workers control. The soviets were not to be theirs until the autumn and the failure of Kornilov's military coup, when Bolshevik sentiment rose up like a wave. In the atmosphere of revolution, without a constituted power and with the war raging, the coup would give the Bolsheviks an opportunity for a temporary majority in the soviets, an opportunity they were to seize. At the Congress of Soviets, Tseretelli, the Menshevik Minister of Posts and Telegraphs, had made a speech in which he remarked that there was no party willing to assume the state power. Lenin, when his chance came to reply, said "There is such a party!"

The Bolsheviks in the capital were not sure of any of this in the early days of the revolution. Before Lenin arrived in April, the Bolshevik press under the direction of Molotov, Kamenev, Stalin, and others was understandably confused and could not decide to what line to take on the Provisional Government. To what extent was it a fulfillment of their Jacobin slogan of the Democratic Dictatorship of Proletariat and Peasantry? And how should the war affect their stance? On his arrival in Petrograd, Lenin surprised them by calling the Provisional Government "capitalist-imperialist." Only a workers' state based on the soviets, he said, could make peace and create "the Commune." Most Bolsheviks were thunderstruck. Mensheviks thought they heard the old voice of Trotskyism and an echo of the idea of the Permanent Revolution. Plekhanov thought Lenin had made himself "the heir to the throne of Bakunin."

On the other hand, the mood of the new government was buoyant. It now took its place defending the revolution with all the most enlightened regimes in the world. When the United States came into the war in April, the Provisional Government could echo the statements of Wilson about the war being one to save the world for democracy. In this spirit it had to accept the autonomy of Finland and Estonia and the claims of the Poles to independence, despite that it did not feel that the Wilsonian idea of national self-determination applied to the lands of the former Russian Empire. It could be argued that Wilson's notion of a war for democracy was close to the idea of a Peace with no Annexations or Indemnities, which the Petrograd Soviet had already advanced. At any rate the Mensheviks and SRs took readily to talking in this way. They said that while they fought for democracy, they also strove for an international conference on peace, called for April in Stockholm. It would finally meet in July, despite the hostility of the allies, with no real results.

At the end of April, Miliukov sent a note to the allies mentioning the obligation of the latter to yield the Straits to Russia. He referred to "war on the old terms." The reference was to the secret treaty of London, 1915, in which Britain promised Russia the Straits in the event of an entente victory. Miliukov's words were was taken by the radical press as an admission of imperialist war aims. German propaganda leaflets distributed at the front had charged that the Russians were not fighting for democracy at all, but for secret treaties that had promised to Russia Constantinople and the Straits. There were huge demonstrations against "Miliukov Dardenelsky." Miliukov had to resign in a general cabinet shake-up. In these extraordinary circumstances, liberalism was thus forced off the stage, never to return. In its place there arose the figure of Aleksandr Kerensky, now elevated from Minister of Interior to War Minister. He had been included in the coalition as a leftist, an SR, and a man of the Soviet. Now that liberalism could no longer carry on, the war had to be won by Kerensky who alone, it was thought, could mobilize the forces of the left. In mid-June he put on a uniform, mounted his touring car, and sent the "Kerensky offensive" into Galicia, to the same part of the front where the Brusilov offensive had made its penetration in 1916. Russian troops quickly took Tarnopol, Galich, and thousands of Austrian prisoners.

The American mission of Elihu Root came to Petrograd to lend its support and discuss a loan to the Provisional Government. All of this was, however, contingent on Russia staying in the war: "No fight, no loan." George Kennan later argued, in his *Russia and the West under Lenin and Stalin*, that the Root Mission made a terrible mistake. Russia should have been permitted to leave the war, and thus spared the October revolution. At any rate, as the offensive rolled on, Kerensky used specially organized shock troops to good effect. General Kornilov had some good luck against bedraggled Austrian forces in Bukovina. But where the Russians came up against the German forces, or units spearheaded by them, they were beaten back. In the bulk of the Russian force, the infantry units, orders had to be approved by soldiers' committees. There were frequent clashes with the officers and even mutinies. Despite the restoration of the death penalty and harsh attempts to keep discipline, forces that were driven off by the Germans did not withdraw in good order, but completely disintegrated. The Russian army was finished. Viewed politically, Kerensky's offensive had pitted all the pro-war forces, including those of the leaders of the Soviet, against troops who would not carry on the fight any longer. Desperate soldiers turned increasingly to those who promised peace, even by means of revolution.

In the beginning of July there were again massive riots as in April. Finland declared its independence, as did the Ukraine. There was another cabinet shake-up, this time bringing Mensheviks and SRs into a government led by Kerensky as Premier. The new combination of left Soviet forces suppressed the July rising and drove the Bolsheviks out of the capital. They accused Lenin of being a German agent. Trotsky, not yet a Bolshevik, pointed out to the government that he was saying the same things as the Bolsheviks and deserved to be persecuted with them. Only Trotsky would have thought to do this. The government obliged by arresting him. Later in the month, the *mezhraiontsy*, the "Interborough Organization," Trotsky's faction, were admitted into the Bolshevik ranks as a group, with recognition of seniority as if they had been Bolsheviks since 1903. The future Minister of Culture Luncharsky, the historian Pokrovsky, the Marxist scholar Riazanov, the Comintern official Manuilsky, diplomats Joffe and Karakhan, and many others of the former Trotskyists now became Bolsheviks. They all got to share the misery and persecution now being meted out to their new party.

Lenin fled across the Finnish border and went to work on an essay to provide a theoretical justification for a socialist revolution in a backward country. The result was *The State and Revolution*, an extended investigation of Marx's ideas about the Paris Commune of 1871. Marx had written *The Civil War in France* to explain why, when locked in a fearful dispute with the anarchist Bakunin over the leadership of the First Workers' International, he nevertheless took the same position as Bakunin in support of the Commune, which had in many ways attempted to crush the state power. Lenin was impressed by Marx's "anarchist" perspective. Maksimov, for the anarchists, was of the opinion that, if Marx had not endorsed the Paris Commune, Marxism would have ended up "in the highways and byways of the labor movement." Lenin decided that the Marxist position of crushing the bourgeois state had been suppressed by the Social Democratic Marxists of his own time, although he had never raised any objection about this prior to 1914. The Dictatorship of the Proletariat in Russia would produce a regime like the Paris Commune, a regime that, in the act of taking power, was initiating in a certain sense the withering away of the state. *The State and Revolution* was not an anarchist document, nor one that gave the slightest nod to anarchism. Even so it was a document that made possible both the conversion of many anarchists to Marxism and a trend in Marxism that the most respected Social Democratic leaders and theorists would consider a fateful concession to anarchism.

After the July rising, the Bolsheviks were driven underground and order restored, but Kerensky still could not find the key to victory. If the liberals had failed and the left had failed, perhaps the army leadership might have the answer. Supreme Commander-in-Chief Brusilov was replaced by General Kornilov, hero of the Kerensky offensive, who was the star of the Moscow State conference in August, at which Plekhanov, Chernov for the SRs, Kropotkin, and others gave stirring speeches. Kornilov argued in effect that the front was in good order but that "we must not lose the war in the rear." It was necessary to close up the Soviet and to rout the defeatist elements. The fall of Riga to the Germans on August 21 put more pressure on Kerensky to bring Kornilov into the government. Negotiations were advanced by inter- mediaries who allowed Kornilov to think that Kerensky would accept him as head of state and offer his own assistance. Kornilov accepted these presumed terms but when Kerensky learned of them he dis- missed Kornilov and placed Petrograd under martial law. Kornilov, who claimed never to have plotted against Kerensky, was indignant and marched his troops on Petrograd. A desperate Kerensky was forced to appeal to the Bolsheviks for help. They obliged and offered their Red Guards for the task, if Kerensky would only arm them and release the detained Bolsheviks from jail. The capital was thus to be defended by the forces of the Soviet and the Bolshevik Red Guards. The Bolshevik railwaymen and telegraphers stopped Kornilov's trains and agitators worked their way among the troops. Soon the march fell apart and Kornilov surrendered.

The failure of the Kornilov affair changed everything. Kerensky no longer appeared as the tribune of the Russian democracy but as one ready to broker a military dictatorship and the suppression of the Soviet. The liberals were suspected of arranging the putsch. They fled. The Left SRs, a faction growing in the SR party since Zimmerwald, now advocating the Bolshevik land program (that is, the old SR pro- gram) openly encouraged the Bolsheviks to take power. The Left SRs would have posts in the first Soviet government up to the peace of Brest Litovsk. Lenin weighed the possibility of changing his tactical line. After the Menshevik and SR forces of the Soviet had driven him into flight in July, he had considered some other slogan to replace "All Power to the Soviets," which now appeared rather ludicrous in view of the fact that it was the Soviet that had driven him and his party out of the capital. Perhaps "All Power to the Factory Committees"? This would have sufficed. All the factory committees would have had to do was to convene a permanent citywide assembly and they would have their new "soviet." It would have been soviet versus soviet. But now the Pet- rograd Soviet, along with Moscow and the other big towns, was actually going Bolshevik in response to the Kornilov revolt. The Bolsheviks were permitted by this to consider the possibility of an insurrection to give them power. Slipping briefly and secretly into town for a meeting on October 10, Lenin made the case to the Bolshevik leaders. He stressed that it was only a temporary opportunity. There was a mutiny in the German fleet; the Bolsheviks must not fall behind. Kerensky might sur- render Petrograd to the Germans (defeatist slogans were now ignored). The peasant war was at its height but might let up. Kerensky might be preparing some new putsch. It was time to take the power. The vote was 10-2, with Lenin's two most trusted exile associates, Zinoviev and Kamenev, voting against him. It was only a commitment to insurrection "in principle." No date was set. It was to be insurrection "at the first suitable opportunity."

The opportunity came as the result of the Germans taking the strategic Moon Islands near the Gulf of Finland that leads to Petrograd. Rumor had it that Kerensky would abandon Petrograd to flee to Moscow. In response to this presumed threat the Soviet formed the Military Revolutionary Committee, led by Trotsky, the newly elected President of the Soviet, in recognition of the same post that he had held in 1905. Trotsky, as a leader of the Bolshevik party, prepared the Soviet to organize defense of the city. Kerensky, it was thought, could not be trusted for the task. The MRC acted in defense of Petrograd against a suspected plot to yield it to the Germans. Kerensky sensed disaster and made a last-ditch attempt to resist. He closed some Bolshevik papers. This gave the MRC the chance to "defend itself" against Kerensky. It did so by a series of tests, issuing orders to see if it rather than the Provisional Government would be obeyed. A garrison conference set up by the MRC, attended by many Bolsheviks, anarchists, and Left SRs, voted to back the Soviet. The MRC ordered the Sestoretsk arms works to deliver 5,000 rifles. Trotsky attended a meeting of regimental committees at the Peter-Paul fortress across the Neva from the Winter Palace and won them for the MRC. Troops from the Peter-Paul took the telegraph office. The revolution was not an incitement to disorder but a defense of an already established soviet order. Historian Alexander Rabinowitch argues that the MRC was defending and only went over to the offensive at 9 p.m. on the night of October 24, a turn that he says can be pinpointed at the moment when it took the Troitsky Bridge over the Neva. Historian Robert Daniels also puts a shift to the offensive at a precise moment, Lenin's arrival at the Bolshevik headquarters at the Smolny institute, after several months' absence, at midnight the same night.

The insurrection was defensive in the sense that the Soviet was defending the capital from the Germans by defending itself from Kerensky. It was a defense of the Soviet power set up in February by Order Number One. To take the power, was it necessary to go over to the offensive? More to the point, was that something that required the agency of Lenin? At 6 p.m. that evening Lenin had sent a note urging the party leadership to "let the Military Revolutionary Committee take the power, or some other institution." Some other institution? Was Lenin entirely abreast of what was going on? It is highly doubtful that he would have chosen the MRC as the preferred vehicle of the revolution. It makes sense to suppose that he would have wanted to make the revolution in the name of the Bolshevik party rather than the Soviet. Trotsky, on the other hand, was actually directing the Soviet in the moves that took power as a member of the Bolshevik party. The Soviet in whose name he was acting was dominated by the Bolsheviks. He had no party other than Lenin's party. And he was sure that Lenin and he were pursuing exactly the same ends. Yet he preferred to do it under the sign of the Soviet rather than the Bolshevik party. Without Trotsky, Lenin probably could not have carried out his plans. He tried to expel Zinoviev and Kamenev, who opposed the insurrection, but was prevented by the rest of the leadership. The Zinoviev-Kamenev position was quite strong, as every meeting demonstrated. Most important, Lenin, except for the most important meetings, was not on the scene.

It was Trotsky, not Lenin, who actually organized and commanded the insurrection on the level of masses and soviets. Lenin came into it when the matter had to be resolved at the level of parties and governments. Any differences on tactics were in the end unimportant. Afterward, Lenin said sheepishly, "Well, well, it can be done that way too. Just take the power." And Trotsky reflected that "we had refused to seize the power by a conspiratorial plot." One could say that the October revolution depended on a bargain between the two men. In winning Lenin, Trotsky got the leadership of a disciplined party and press; in winning Trotsky, Lenin got the revolution.

At 6:50 p.m. on October 25, a 20-minute ultimatum was given to the Winter Palace. Kerensky had fled the city a few hours before. The ultimatum was ignored. The *Aurora* and some other destroyers came up alongside the building and fired a few blanks and then some live rounds. At 2 a.m. on October 26, MRC troops finally arrested the Provisional Government. Across town, the Second Congress of Soviets was read a proclamation deposing the government and the Menshevik-SR leadership of the assembled soviets and putting all authority in the hands of the Congress. The proclamation promised "in the name of the Petrograd Soviet" an immediate peace, land to the peasants, democratization of the armed forces, workers control, a Constituent Assembly, and self-determination to the nationalities. There was nothing in the first decrees about the Bolshevik party. The program, taken as a whole, was called the Soviet Power. But at the time when it came into being no one, not even those who called it into being could know exactly what it was, and what carrying out its promises would entail.

CHAPTER 6

The Civil War and War Communism, 1918–1921

The first actions of the Soviet state kindled intense conflict, not only with domestic enemies but also with allies in the struggles of 1917 who quickly turned into enemies. Before the year was out, these had been joined by the entente powers intervening on several fronts in a desperate attempt to get Russia back into the war. In response the Bolsheviks, who had got to power by means of what the German socialist parliamentarian Otto Rühle called a "pacifist putsch," turned on a dime and raised armies to defend the revolution. More than that, they proclaimed their intention to make Soviet Russia the center of a cosmic campaign to overthrow all the imperialist governments engaged in the war on either side and to encourage their colonial subjects to revolt against them. Acting in such a way as to confront the whole world might have seemed at first to promise a quick end to the Soviet power, but in fact the opposition of former allies caused the Bolsheviks to rally around the party and even around the party leadership against criticism in the party. Bitter opposition faced by the revolution on so many fronts had the effect of cancelling sensible hesitations, overcoming reasonable doubts, and making the revolutionaries more steely and determined. Curiously, the new Time of Troubles was a godsend for the Communist dictatorship in the highly militarized form that evolved in those terrible years of civil war. None of its contours could have been foreseen in any blueprint. From the start everything was forced by the harshest of circumstances.

The October revolution had been made in the name of the maximalism of 1917: a separate peace, "black repartition" of the land, workers' control, self-determination for the nationalities. Many of those who made the revolution thought not that they were establishing Soviet power as a new order but that they were overthrowing state power as such and clearing away the obstacles to the soviets, factory committees, peasant communes, house committees, and other organizations tossed up by the spontaneity of the masses. One could say that the prevailing mood was a kind of anarchism. On their way to majorities in the soviets, the Bolsheviks tried not to run afoul of anarchist sentiment. Many prominent anarchists joined the Bolshevik party, as many anarchists and syndicalists abroad joined Communist parties. The Manifesto of the Communist International, issued in 1919, railed against the "state socialists" in western countries who had supported the war. It promised to small countries that the proletarian revolution would free the productive forces "from the tentacles of the national states." Even so, as soon as the Bolsheviks took power, they could not help but run up against their maximalist allies of 1917.

One of the last acts in concert with their allies on the left was the dispersal of the Constituent Assembly in January 1918. The SRs rather than the Bolsheviks had the biggest poll with 16 million votes, about 40 percent. They won the countryside while the Bolsheviks took the big city labor vote of 10 million, about 25 percent. The Mensheviks practically disappeared as an electoral party with a little over a million and the Kadets found themselves in similar condition with two million. This was an extremely radical result, much more radical than the elections to the second Duma, the one that Stolypin had to close down in 1907. The composition of that Duma was evenly divided between parties of the right and the left, with sizable groupings of Kadets and Octobrists. In the Constituent Assembly, the liberals and the right were reduced to a negligible quantity. The SR leadership, sensing its weak position in the presumed leadership of the presumably sovereign body, gave no indication of an attempt to undo the result of the peasant war of 1917. However, it also vowed that there would be no separate peace with the Central Powers. It deplored the peace negotiations initiated by the Bolsheviks. The SRs and Mensheviks said they would have continued to meet with western socialists to talk peace, as with the Stockholm process in 1917, but they insisted that for the time being no break with the entente could be contemplated. Could they possibly have got the troops to fight again where Kerensky had failed?

Anarchist sailors in the guard grumbled about this and finally, after a marathon session on the first day, closed the Assembly. The Bolsheviks made no effort to reconvene it, saying that the Assembly did not truly reflect opinion on the countryside because the lists for the election did not reflect the split in the SR party. In the Baltic fleet, in Kazan, and in Petrograd, where the lists did reflect the split, the Left SRs won overwhelmingly. It seems intuitive that the peasants, who had taken the land and wanted peace, would have voted for the Left SRs, who had the Bolshevik position on land and peace, rather than the Right SRs who had abandoned their old land program to continue the war. At any rate, the central point for the Bolsheviks was that the Constituent Assembly had already been superseded by the Soviet Power, which represented a "higher form." From the standpoint of the SR leadership, the Assembly would at some point have had to try to raise troops to suppress the soviets, in an effort to take things back to where they had stood in 1917. Could they have avoided a separate peace? Apparently few Russians thought so. There was no protest against the dispersal of the Assembly. Nevertheless, there is no denying that this was a desperate act taken against Western-style parliamentary democracy by the united forces of the Soviet Power.

Dispersing the Constituent Assembly did, however, make it possible to accept the onerous peace imposed by the Germans at Brest-Litovsk in March 1918, according to which the Germans separated the Ukraine, the Baltics, and the Caucasus. Romania had already taken Bessarabia. Soviet Russia was reduced to roughly the lands of the old Moscow principality. Peace with Germany broke up the Bolshevik bloc with the left SRs and almost split the party itself, with a "War Party" around Nikolai Bukharin complaining bitterly about the betrayal of the revolution. The War party had extended the case for the maximalism of 1917 by urging that the revolution march on Germany behind Soviet bayonets. Lenin, in the minority, said it was all playing with phrases and, worst of all, playing with phrases about war. Trotsky temporarily headed the war off by offering the slogan "Neither War Nor Peace," that is, declare an end to hostilities without a signed peace. This verbal trickery won the day and became policy. Lenin disdained it but it saved him from the War Party. However, the Germans refuted it by marching on and taking Kiev in a matter of days. This time the peace terms were harsher than the original ones, which had left to Russia Latvia and Estonia. The Germans absorbed Russian Poland, Lithuania, Latvia, and Estonia and sponsored protectorates in Finland, Ukraine, and Georgia. The embattled Bolshevik government was forced to move to Moscow.

Bukharin, who had influence in the Moscow party organization, appealed to radicals unhappy with the peace, with the fact that not much industry had been nationalized, and with the policy of shifting support, for the sake of efficiency and centralization, from the factory committees to the trade unions. The peace had alienated the Left SRs, who resented the loss of the Ukraine. Workers' control served for the moment as a substitute for seizure of the factories, but favoring the trade unions had the effect of recruiting some Mensheviks who became born-again Bolsheviks, while it angered the anarchists. Bukharin added things up and decided to speak out in his journal *Kommunist* for a constituency on the left of the party that regretted losing these allies. He packaged the protest in a theory to the effect that the revolution had failed as a socialist project and only produced "state capitalism." If the "Left Communists" could not be reconciled, the party might split into maximalist and defeatist sub-parties. But Lenin was able to defeat Bukharin and the Left by arguing that "state capitalism" in the form of an imitation of the German war economy would actually be a splendid model for a future Soviet Communism. He argued this in an article, "Left Wing Childishness and Petty Bourgeois Mentality" (not to be confused with his essay of 1920, "Left Wing Communism: An Infantile Disorder"). Faced with a party dispute that might move Lenin to write and argue him into the ground, Bukharin relented.

An important point had been made. Lenin had forcefully contended and got the party to accept that the Soviet regime was not to be a socialist experiment but a state capitalist economy. That would have been his initial preference, that is, if there had been peace. Almost immediately, however, the Bolsheviks were forced into a civil war with foreign intervention. The outbreak of civil war made the regime into something quite different, a collectivist military dictatorship under what was later called War Communism. Nationalizations of industrial property spread rapidly in the spring and summer, mostly against the wishes of the regime. It abolished money, paid wages in kind, provided lodgings free of rent and utilities, and collected virtually no taxes. This was the Spartan "barracks" regime under which the civil war would be fought.

The Entente powers recoiled at the thought of Russia leaving the war and the simultaneous repudiation of all debts owed by the old regime. They worked feverishly to find a way to overthrow the Bolsheviks and reconstitute the eastern front against Germany. It proved possible for them to arm some Cossack bands in the south who defied Soviet rule, but they did not promise much militarily. Britain and France themselves found it hard to raise troops and harder to cooperate with each other across the separate zones they established in December 1917. On the other hand the revolt of a Czech legion of prisoners of war suddenly presented an opportunity of setting up a

Siberian front. These troops were from Czech units of the army of the Habsburg Empire who, having been taken prisoner by the Russians, were won over to the prospect of an independent Czechoslovakia, as envisioned by the allies. The Russians were moving them to the Far East along the Trans-Siberian rail line for subsequent embarkation for Europe to fight against the Habsburg monarchy, according to plans laid down in 1917. They predictably came into conflict with the local Soviet authorities at stations on the way east. They moved down the line, deposing by force local soviets until they showed up in Vladivostok. From there the French sent them back to the west as a vanguard for Japanese forces that eventually took over Siberia up to Lake Baikal. All this to bolster the allied war effort.

There was powerful pressure on President Wilson to support the intervention, in a spirit quite opposite to the generous treatment that he had promised Soviet Russia in the Fourteen Points speech of January 1918. Wilson, in an effort to prevent a separate Russo-German peace, had tried to make common cause with Bolshevism. He had defined American war aims in such a way as to appeal to those who welcomed the proclamations from Stockholm and Zimmerwald and the appeal of the Petrograd Soviet for "a peace without annexations or indemnities." But Wilson was also worried about the Japanese, who cared nothing for the restoring of the Russian front against Germany and sought only to establish a sphere of influence in Siberia. Wilson, under this pressure, broke down and consented to send troops to fight in Russia, in the east and the north.

When the Czechs' drive to the west reached Samara on the Volga, the way was clear for the SRs to set up a "government of the Constituent Assembly," promising to unite the democracy against Bolshevism and the Germans and to reestablish the Entente's eastern front in the war. The Bolsheviks were not able to test this regime in battle until August. For most of the spring they had been uncertain about German intentions and even flirted with the bizarre idea, floated by some unofficial representatives of the Entente and the Americans, of accepting allied aid to resume the fight against the Germans, "taking rifles and potatoes from the bandits of Anglo-French imperialism," in Lenin's colorful phrase. At the same time they did not want to provoke the Germans into a march on Moscow, as they might by failing to disarm the Czechs. The German advance did not materialize, perhaps because of the distraction provided by the allied offensive on the western front.

Peace with Germany meant war with the SRs and their allies. Things were made still worse by the disruption of food supplies to the cities and the withholding of grain by the peasants. The Bolsheviks did not hesitate to organize Committees of the Poor Peasants to seize the grain by force, including that which might have been consumed by the peasants. The compulsory grain requisitions, said Lenin, marked the point at which the revolution passed over to a socialist phase, despite everything he had said about state capitalism. For their part, the peasants had been favorable to the "Bolsheviks" who had urged them to take the land instead of waiting for the Constituent Assembly, but now they resented the "Communists" who took the grain from them. In July 1918, the SRs, with French encouragement, rose in Moscow, took control of Yaroslavl, assassinated Count Mirbach, the German ambassador, and several prominent Bolsheviks, and fired at and wounded Lenin. As the Czechs and Whites descended on Ekaterinburg, the local soviet shot the tsar and his family. From the west the troops of the Red Army, organized by Trotsky with many tsarist officers (*spetsy*, or bourgeois specialists) in command and a commissar apparatus in control of them, arrived on the Volga. The first red victory, an artillery duel at Sviazhsk, was hailed as the "Valmy" of the Russian revolution, recalling the first time the French revolution had defended itself with armed forces. The SR government moved back to Ufa and then to Omsk as the reds captured Kazan and Samara.

The Bolsheviks were on the move against what Louis Fischer later called the "Little Intervention," the intervention to bring Russia back into the war. The SRs had bent every effort to make this a revolutionary war in the name of the democracy of 1917, a war in behalf of the allies, the most progressive nations in the world, against German militarism and its Bolshevik satraps. But this noble cause could not survive the victory of the allies in the west. When the western and Balkan fronts collapsed in November 1918, Admiral Kolchak, with encouragement from British officers attached to his staff, arrested the SR leaders and made himself Supreme Ruler with dictatorial powers. The allies who went to Versailles to make peace had to find a policy to deal with the fait accompli. At this point, the allied campaign turned into a Big Intervention, one whose end could only be the overthrow of Soviet power. Events with a similar political coloring transpired in the north.

At the news of the armistice, Lenin remarked, in a mixture of Russian and German, "Na nas idyot das Weltkapital" (Now the forces of world capital will descend upon us). But this was not to be a formidable force, not nearly as formidable as the remaining White armies. There was in fact an ephemeral allied project in the spring of 1919 for a conference at Prinkipo to make peace among the Russian factions. But the collapse of the project was overshadowed by the rise of a Soviet Republic in Hungary. The Hungarian Socialists made a desperate attempt to evade the partition that the Paris conferees had in mind for the Hungarian lands. With the aid of the Hungarian Communists, they formed a Hungarian Soviet Republic as a ploy to draw in Soviet support for a revolt against the peace. This was a gamble on the chance that the Soviets could defeat the White forces and march on Hungary. Lenin could not hide his naive enthusiasm for the Communist victory in the "land of the poets." In the end the Hungarian regime was overrun by Romanian troops before the Red Army could help. Yet a note of "national bolshevism" had been sounded, a suggestion to all the defeated states that a Communist revolution might be a device to defy the Entente by means of a nationalist rally.

The White generals were to have allied support in their last attempts to unseat the Bolsheviks. These campaigns all began to run aground in 1919. By summer, the British, faced with unrest in India, Egypt, and Ireland, decided to drop all efforts in Russia. There was a mutiny in the French fleet near Odessa in April. By summer the British took most of their troops out of the Caucasus and carried off almost all of the Russian merchant fleet. The Whites made a concerted last effort that came close to success. Kolchak got as far as Perm with around 125,000 troops in his attempt to link up with the northern forces. In the south forces led by Denikin got as far as Orel, threatening Tula, which would have threatened Moscow, but were defeated by a coalition of reds and anarchist troops led by Nestor Makhno. Yudenich overran the Baltic coast and bore down on Petrograd in October 1919, taking Tsarskoe Selo, and prompting Trotsky to race to the former capitol to organize a fight in its city streets. Yudenich failed to get the British fleet to bombard the city to prepare his entrance. This would in any case have been futile if the Whites had not won everywhere else.

All the fronts broke shortly. Kolchak was defeated near Omsk and then captured by the Czechs and turned over, with French approval, to the Soviets, and shot. Yudenich backed off from Petrograd. The campaigns wound down in 1920. The last phase was the Polish invasion of Ukraine. Marshal Piłsudski had attacked Vilna and Lvov in 1919, but he was reluctant to do more for the Whites, in view of their nationalist commitment to Russia One and Undivided. But after the Whites were driven off in defeat, Piłsudski and his forces, with French encouragement, poured into the Ukraine, taking Kiev in April 1920. He wanted a Poland as it had existed before the partitions of the eighteenth century, even a "Poland from Sea to Sea" (from the Baltic to the Black Sea). He was quickly driven out of the Ukraine and Red forces pursued him to Warsaw, where they were themselves stopped in August 1920. The Soviets had to accept a line drawn by the Treaty of Riga that included sections of Lithuania, Belorussia (today's Belarus), and Ukraine as parts of Poland.

It was a dramatic finish to a struggle of continental scope that cost the lives of millions, almost on a scale with the losses incurred in the Great War itself. Some historians take the view that a civil war of such a scope could not have happened without the allied intervention that supported it. Winston Churchill confronted this question at the end of his history of the war, in a volume called *The Aftermath*. Was it worthwhile, he asked, to have incurred the seemingly permanent wrath of the new Soviet state without carrying away a victory? His answer was that it was indeed worthwhile even to have lost in Russia, because the Communist "plague bacillus" was thereby kept out of central Europe, where it had threatened to spread, through Hungary and rump Austria, into Bavaria, and even into Berlin.

It was an extraordinary introduction into the community of nations. Soviet propaganda for decades afterward would remind the West of the mould having been set in their relations by the horrible events of these years. Khrushchëv said he was reminded of the civil war and allied intervention as he contemplated putting missiles into Cuba in 1962. Soviet Communism has now passed from the scene and all this is a matter for historians. Yet perhaps we can better understand the emergence of the Communist idea if we see it in the context of world war and civil war. At the end of this period the Bolsheviks were certainly not the same people they were in the years when their most urgent task was getting out a daily paper. They had learned to command troops with commissars, to send men to die, to shoot those who refused their orders, to apply pressure in the most direct and brutal sense. Communism was formed by these habits and practices.

Some indication of the process is given by the strange result of the trade union debate conducted in 1920. It began with a discussion of Trotsky's wartime militarization of the railways. These measures worked splendidly but provoked a conflict with the trade union leadership that Trotsky had to overcome. His success with the railways encouraged him to argue for militarization of labor as a policy for the whole economy. Against this his opponents mustered a vast array. It included the former Left Communists of 1918; the military opposition who had fought against his use of *spetsy*; Tomsky as head of the Soviet trade unions; Zinoviev, faithful associate of Lenin through years of exile who opposed Trotsky perhaps for having led the October insurrection while he, Zinoviev, had advised against; and a Workers' Opposition that advocated letting the trade unions run the whole economy in a "congress of producers." Lenin hung back and regularly supported Trotsky. Stalin supported Lenin. In fact, Lenin did not have a position of his own on the matter for several months, only a vague feeling of unease at Trotsky's power rising so suddenly. Eventually he worked out a rationale for opposing Trotsky: the trade unions ought not to be under military discipline; they should be "schools for Communism," led by the party in the factory, independent of the state and the army.

Trotsky appeared in this reckoning as the man of the state and Lenin the man of the party. Bukharin at one point asked Lenin whether his distrust of the state power made sense if theirs was a workers' state. "What kind of state do we have?" Bukharin asked mischievously. A flustered Lenin replied: "A workers' state." But then he corrected himself: "A workers' state that relies on the peasantry," and later, "a workers' state with bureaucratic distortions." One could see the reflexes of the Jacobin Lenin still uncomfortable with the proletarian revolution according to the idea of Permanent Revolution. Or perhaps it is much simpler: Lenin was just worrying about Trotsky's having too much power gathered in his person.

The debate was raging, with no less than eight platform factions having their say, when news came in that the sailors of Kronstadt had risen in revolt against the Soviet regime. It was said that they called for "soviets without Communists." While the Bolsheviks had been debating the ideal economy, the food situation in the capital had got so bad as to cause a general strike with which the sailors were now in sympathy. At about the same time, at the end of 1920 and beginning of 1921, a peasant revolt in Tambov province south of Moscow raged among tens of thousands of insurgents. It spread down the Volga basin and took months to suppress. The Bolsheviks had to drop the debate and put down the risings with force. This they managed to do, but the victory caused them no joy as opposed to their other feats. The Kronstadt sailors had been their most fervent supporters, the "vanguard" of the revolutionary forces of 1917. And this victory came as a climax to a string of victories over the maximalists of 1917: left SRs, anarchists, and Left Communists who opposed Brest-Litovsk; peasants who resisted compulsory grain requisitions; enlisted men and noncoms in the army who opposed the command of the *spetsy*; anarchist workers who favored the factory committees over the trade unions. Some thought that in conquering the counterrevolution, the Bolsheviks had conquered the revolution as well. It seemed no exaggeration to suppose that a party to the left of the Bolsheviks might have a good chance to push them aside, or to cause a split in their ranks. That was what made this debate and all subsequent debates so urgent, the feeling that every dispute might cause a split and that a split would result in a new civil war.

The only answer, said Lenin, was to compromise on every front. Everything must be done to get food for the cities and to placate the peasantry. The Tenth Party Congress therefore resolved to implement a New Economic Policy replacing the compulsory grain requisitions with a small tax in kind, permitting the peasants to sell the surplus on the free market. Lenin said it was a return to his old idea of state capitalism after the utopias of War Communism. He admitted it was a retreat, even a great one, "a peasant Brest," but the party would tighten up its own regime, ban factions, and hold the fortress of its dictatorship until the clouds passed. These were all thought of as pragmatic, really forced, decisions that did not touch principle and could be reversed when things got better. In fact, however, taken together, they were to comprise the permanent institutional face of Soviet Communism, at least until a new revolution from above would reject them as too soft.

CHAPTER 7

From Lenin to Stalin, 1921–1928

The regime of revolutionary Russia that emerged after the Bolshevik victory in the civil war was a kind of paradox. On the one hand it was a new world, a place where the most extreme ideas of nineteenth-century socialism were presumably to have a living experiment. On the other, it was a world that its creators saw as impossible. They could not have been Marxists if they truly believed that a backward country could leap into socialism without a more or less drawn-out interval of capitalism. Russian Marxists had lived with this paradox since the suggestion of Marx, in his letter to Vera Zasulich of 1881, that the impossible would indeed be possible if a Russian revolution were accompanied by a genuinely proletarian revolution in an advanced capitalist country, presumably Germany. Soviet Russia was not to be the land around which the world revolution would be organized. It had merely acted as a trigger for a much larger project that, once it got under way, would subordinate Russia to a more advanced country that would become the real leader of the socialist revolution. When the Russian Communists organized the Communist international in 1919, they conducted its sessions in German, in anticipation of the salvation of their desperate 1917 revolt against war. In the meantime, they had to build the institutions of worker-peasant Russia, which the German industrialist and politician Walter Rathenau characterized pityingly as a "rigidly oligarchic agrarian republic."

At the same time, the Bolsheviks set out to reorganize the vast Russian empire. A federal structure began to take shape immediately under the guiding hand of Stalin, the party's nationalities expert. He was committed to maintaining a core of Russian primacy among the nationalities liberated from tsarism. After the end of the civil war these included the Ukraine, the Caucasus, Central Asia, and the Far Eastern regions, to be governed as Soviet Republics more or less autonomous in much of their domestic life. Non-Russians were almost half of the 140 million Soviet citizens. By 1922, citizens of the Union of Soviet Socialist Republics were grouped into nine Union Republics, alongside numerous autonomous republics (ASSRs) and less-populous, smaller autonomous territories. Communists quickly arrived at the device of encouraging a measure of local nationalism in the Muslim areas as a check on broader Islamic solidarity.

The Communist party was their link to the all-Union structure. After it banned the Mensheviks and anarchists in 1921, it had no rivals at the head of a one-party dictatorship. The Dictatorship of the Proletariat that it directed denied a vote in elections for Soviet institutions to millions of people, priests, nobles, bourgeois, and kulaks. It gave more weight to the vote of a worker than a peasant. It decreed separation of church and state. It confiscated church lands and many of the possessions of churches themselves. It suppressed religious schools and put difficulties in the way of publication of devotional literature. In the name of militant materialism, atheist propaganda tried to fill the gap. The League of the Godless, the *bezbozhniki*, agitated for atheist perspectives. Against the attractions of church services and holiday rites, it offered instead the *klub*, where one could read enlightened material, play chess, and partake of social life. Museums of cults were set up, in which one could view exhibits, not always very subtle or sophisticated, of various unpleasant or ridiculous religious practices. In the spirit of Byzantine Caesaro-Papism the church tended to bear it all with a patient shrug. Despite everything, it enjoined the faithful to support the Bolshevik state in the name of Mother Russia.

This did not cause the government to relent in its effort to wean family life from religion. It abolished church marriage and set up little secular marriage temples. Divorce was legalized and encouraged when conditions and desires seemed to warrant it. The distinction between legitimate and illegitimate children disappeared. Abortion was available on demand. Ideas that we consider enlightened on many matters concerning love and marriage became common features of the new society. The professions were opened to women and the party encouraged propaganda that depicted the life of the housewife as one of drudgery and privation.

These policies opened many doors and closed some others. Women were *never*, even to the end of the regime in 1991, particularly prominent in politics and government as, for example, they are today in the

British House of Commons. Liberation from family responsibilities also liberated many men from responsibilities toward their children. Often they did not have progressive attitudes toward sharing custody of their children and subsequently increased the burdens of single mothers. Poor families broke up. The streets in the towns were filled with urchins, who were regarded as a nuisance, much as gypsy children are today. They pressed their faces to windows of restaurants to watch the patrons dine, and no real effort was made to deliver them back to their families. They wandered around, sometimes in packs, and found their way, in fortunate cases, to factory work. This was not a utopia for them.

Even with all the difficulties of life in Russia, it occupied a place alongside Weimar Berlin in the world's cultural vanguard. Part of this, oddly, was because of some brilliant émigrés who, despite exile, made an impact on world culture in Russia's name. The philosopher Nikolai Berdyaev, exiled in 1922, wrote penetrating works on Russia's unique cultural history and linked the Russian religious past to current Soviet perspectives, in his view a continuity from the Third Rome to the Third International. Novelist Mikhail Bulgakov began work on his internationally famous novel of ideas, *The Master and Margarita*, later to be suppressed in Stalin's time. Mikhail Rostovtsev wrote historical works on the Ukrainians and on contacts of Russia with the world of classical antiquity. His work on ancient Rome made him a reputation among Western ancient historians. George Vernadsky was the spokesman for the Eurasian school of historians and philologists whose works on Kiev Rus and Russia's steppe heritage were discussed in Chapter 1.

Sergei Eisenstein's films were acclaimed in Russia and in the West. *The Battleship Potemkin* (1926) is still studied in film schools and frequently called one of the greatest films in cinema history. Eisenstein professed a doctrine of film editing called montage, which he claimed to derive from Hegelian dialectic, wherein the director uses action on the scene to create a succession of visual conflicts, often in the arrangement of crowd scenes. Dziga Vertov's *Kino-Nedelya* (Cinema Week) pioneered a kind of cinema verité newsreel style. He shot the famous reenacted crowd scenes of the revolution that one often sees in today's documentaries. The masses became the heroes of Soviet cinema.

Soviet writers and poets represented the phenomenon, unique in Russian experience, of an intelligentsia that agreed with the state. Isaac Babel wrote his wonderful Odessa stories about the Jewish gangster Benya Krik and his various adventures. Novelists Ilf and Petrov told tall tales with a Soviet moral. Soviet poets read their works to large audiences and sometimes scrawled them on the walls in public places. The anarchist Victor Serge describes his first meeting with the poet Sergei Esenin: "I met him in a seedy café. Over-powdered, over-painted women, leaning on the marble slabs, cigarettes between their fingers, drank coffee made from roasted oats. Men, clad in black leather, frowning and tight-lipped, with heavy revolvers at the belts, had their arms around the women's waists. These fellows knew what it was to live rough, knew the taste of blood, the painful impact of a bullet in the flesh, and it all made them appreciative of the poems, incanted and almost sung, whose violent images jostled each other as though in a fight." The literary scene featured disputes between Acmeists who sought a pure vision of the world and Futurists who wanted to make a new poetic language. The most widely acclaimed poet was Vladimir Mayakovsky, for whose work Lenin did not care in the slightest. Mayakovsky wrote stirringly of his Soviet patriotism, as in his "Lines on a Soviet Passport." Or, occasionally he wrote commercial jingles: "Where can you get for your money, the very finest macaroni? Why, in the Moscow food stores."

Enthusiasm ran to the point that some were moved to proclaim that they could create in Soviet Russia a new proletarian culture. But Lenin never took this seriously. Soviet Russia would do well, he thought, to imitate Western culture. The revolution had not and could not produce a truly new and socialist society. Soviet education itself was crucially dependant on bourgeois specialists ("spetsy") who cared little for Communism. And we must remember, he liked to say, that "we are dragging behind us our peasant cart."

The suppression of the Kronstadt and Tambov rebellions coincided with the proclamation of the New Economic Policy (NEP). This provided that, after the exaction from the peasant of a small tax in kind, he would be allowed to sell the rest of his crop on the market to an independent trader. The party retreated from the countryside, holding on to its bastions in the industrial commanding heights of the economy. It also signed a trade treaty with Britain that gave to the Soviets their first de facto recognition. Nikolai Ustrialov, an ex-Kadet who had fought with the armies of Kolchak in Siberia, reflected on these circumstances from his Manchurian exile. Ustrialov concluded that the Russian revolution had reached its Thermidor, its crucial turn to the right, just as the French had with the fall of the Jacobins in 1794. The Russian revolution had been an anarchic process with which the Bolsheviks had gone along to destroy and disperse the old Russian Empire. But as the Bolsheviks assumed the state power they had to end the anarchy, gather in the Russian lands, return to world politics and the world economy, and even one day, Ustrialov thought, restore private property. The anarchist and internationalist Bolshevism of 1917 of necessity had to be replaced by National Bolshevism. Hegel was superior to Marx: the real actors in world history were not classes, but nations. The NEP was the surest sign. Under its rules the sturdy smallholder, the petty trader, and the former tsarist "bourgeois specialist" bureaucrat would form a constituency for a Russian Thermidor.

Ustrialov spoke with eloquence for the enemies of the revolution. He was not alone in trying to see the Russian revolution through the lens of the French revolution. The historian Albert Mathiez, who was to complete by 1922 an influential history of the French revolution, made a case for the identification of Bolshevism with the Jacobins of 1793–1794, "two dictatorships born of civil war and foreign war, dictatorships of class, using the same means, terror, compulsory requisitions and taxes, and proposing in the last resort a single goal, the transformation of society, not merely the Russian or the French, but the universal society." For these views Mathiez was called by the novelist Romain Rolland "the savant-archpriest of the cult of Robespierre." Mathiez supposed that the Russian Thermidor could only result from a split between Lenin and Trotsky. No such split was to materialize. But Trotsky frankly granted that a Thermidor had been passed by the transition to the NEP, except that in this case the Bolsheviks-Jacobins themselves had carried it out.

Ustrialov was certainly right that the Soviet power of 1917, for which the revolutionaries had fought during the civil war, had been completely transformed by the process of national consolidation and defense. No more an anarchic dissolution of the Russian state, it would henceforth be in the grip of the Bolshevik dictatorship. Ustrialov supposed that, as the French Thermidor had led quickly to Bonapartism, so too would the Russian revolution produce at some point a kind of "Caesarist" leader. Perhaps if Ustrialov was right, he was right not just in the case of the statist Bolsheviks but in general in his assertion that Russia's choice was between authoritarianism of the left or right. Could the disintegration of the Russian territorial state have been halted by a regime of the Constituent Assembly? If it was to continue the war, the Assembly would have had to break the soviets. No doubt some new Kornilov would have been necessary for this. The pattern could be observed in the White regimes' relations with their military leaders, even in the case of the regime of the Constituent Assembly in Samara. Men on horseback had pushed aside the democratic elements in all the White governments. Aside from the question of the war, could the Russian democracy have stopped the centripetal tendencies set in motion by the events of 1917 by any other means than a new authoritarianism? Had the Bolsheviks not defeated the Kronstadt idea of soviets without parties, surely it would have been defeated all the same.

The Bolsheviks did not know how to take the doctrine of National Bolshevism. On the one hand it helped their relations with many émigrés who were enjoined by Ustrialov to give up their plotting in the Paris cafés and return to help Russia rebuild under the Bolsheviks. On the other hand, they had to wonder whether Ustrialov had not been right. They repeated to themselves with less than full conviction that NEP was a tactic and not an evolution.

True enough, the suppression of the Kronstadt revolt meant that victory over the counterrevolution was also in effect victory over the revolution. The maximalism of 1917 in its many forms now lay beneath the boot of a new iron-hard Bolshevism such as the Cold War literature used to see in prospect from the time Lenin penned *What Is to Be Done?* in 1902. War Communism had blunted and weakened the idea of Soviet Power because the Soviet Central Executive had expelled from the soviets any party that sided with the Whites. This would have been easily justifiable to anyone who wanted to see the Soviet Power victorious in the civil war. At the same time, one could not call the Soviet Power democratic if it denied the workers a choice of party representation. If it was a one-party dictatorship, it was no longer a democracy.

Could one even call the Communist party democratic in its inner life? The relatively open Communist party policy discussion, under the rubric of democratic centralism, which had been the rule even in the days of revolution and civil war, now gave way to a tighter regime. There were purges of presumed opportunists and careerists who were said to have come into the party only as they sensed that it would win. There were exchanges of party cards to weed them out. But according to what criteria was the process to be governed? Did the party have a "sincere-ometer," as the Italian Socialist Serrati had once taunted Lenin in regard to membership in the Comintern? Lenin's response to Serrati was characteristic: "We must find this sincere-ometer!" As the party set about to cleanse its ranks in 1921–1922, it emerged that by default its most reliable sincere-ometer was status as an "old Bolshevik." This could not be one who had slipped into the party when it was on the verge of power, but only one who had fought faithfully in exile in the days when no one listened and faith was tested. No one at the time dared to apply this criterion to someone like Trotsky or the other *mezhraiontsy* who had fused in 1917, but the implication was nonetheless present, awaiting an occasion.

Lenin saw this clearly but envisioned no alternative. He was aware that Trotsky and the other former non-Bolsheviks could be bruised by the new party institutions. Yet, as his conduct during the trade union debate clearly indicated, he did not view with displeasure the putting of obstacles in the way of Trotsky. Not that he did not value him highly, in some ways more highly than any of the other leaders. Nevertheless, he seems to have feared that Trotsky might make himself a force in the party that could not be resisted. Indeed, in view of the role Trotsky had played in the events of October, he might even with a certain justice have arrogated to himself the vocation of the true voice of the revolution. Lenin was ready to make common cause with anyone in the effort to preserve the party's prerogative against any individual, no matter how brilliant. That is, against any *other* individual.

At the same time, the Bolshevik regime of the Tenth Party Congress was understood to be a new institutional departure. The party was fashioning for itself a new administrative and political apparatus. The party purge was to be done through the Central Control Commission, which would carry out the exchange of party cards. This was added to the Workers and Peasants Inspectorate (*rabkrin*), which since 1919 had been charged with supervision of the half million or so former tsarist officials now employed by the Soviet government. If a postal inspector was permitting the insertion of anti-Bolshevik leaflets or White émigré publications into the daily post, he was to be exposed and dismissed.

Obviously the party leader in charge of supervising these activities would have enormous power concentrated in his hands. Until his death in 1918, the clear choice would have been Jacob Sverdlov, a Bolshevik and a close associate of Lenin since 1902. He had been a faithful and efficient executor of the directives of the leadership, including its instructions to what were later called "the organs," the police forces. According to recent research, he probably had a hand in approving the execution of the Tsar and his family. Sverdlov would have been thought best for the job. But now that he was gone, the next in line was Iosif Vissarionovich Dzugashvili (Stalin), a member of the top leadership for many years, a Politburo member, and Commissar of Nationalities. It is worth noting that Stalin had for years been an active "committeeman," working in the illegal party apparatus within Tsarist Russia, carrying out the distribution of the paper and other clandestine functions at great personal risk while the leadership of the party published its paper from abroad. A profound gulf separated the experiences of the leadership in exile and the committeemen in Russia.

In view of his experience, it made sense to the leaders of the party to trust Stalin with all his posts, to which were added in April 1922 the post of General Secretary. They knew that these were levers that could be used unscrupulously in the disputes among the most ambitious leaders. He who was surprised by this knew nothing about politics. They thought it best, therefore, to put confidence in someone who was not particularly prominent or popular, someone with modest pretensions and expectations, one who had not written crucial documents or articles in any important party dispute and who had little pretension to a mastery of theory, who nevertheless knew how to apply pressure downward in the interest of the Politburo. For this role Stalin was perfect. He could be trusted to carry out the will of the party's true leaders without any threat to the equilibrium among them as individuals. No one envied or begrudged his powers and responsibilities. In fact, to invest him with them was a sign not only that he was trusted but also that he was underestimated.

It would not be correct to say, however, that in the coming years that saw his rise to supreme power, Stalin merely manipulated the apparatus of bureaucratic power (the "Leninist gadgets," as historian and Stalin biographer Isaac Deutscher calls them), while the ineffectual party intellectuals argued the fine points of theory. Stalin got the power because he maneuvered with skill in every policy debate for the next seven years, maintaining a shifty centrist position, in some ways similar to the way Lenin did. For some reason this reassured others as to his lack of ambition. This occurred while the more brilliant leaders, Trotsky, Zinoviev, Kamenev, and Bukharin, fought among themselves with increasing passion, either leaving Stalin alone or seeking his support against each other.

The issues were real enough. As soon as NEP became the economic line, there was a struggle to define it. Finance Minister Sokolnikov, who took credit for the Anglo-Soviet trade treaty of 1921, which allowed a kind of détente between the two countries, seized on Lenin's remark to the effect that NEP was a return to the "state capitalism" of 1918. He offered his own version of state capitalism. The Soviet economy must be integrated by degrees with the world economy. The state monopoly of foreign trade must be relaxed, so that Russians and foreigners could conduct normal commerce. Soviet industry must be put on a basis of *khozraschyot* (self-sufficiency). Trotsky gagged on these ideas. In a workers' state, he insisted, industry must be favored, or soon the Soviets would have to buy their steel from the imperialists. On this as in other matters, Lenin hung back, but on balance he favored the position of Sokolnikov. Lloyd George was following up the trade treaty with plans for a general European conference at Genoa in 1922 to which the Soviets were to be invited. Sokolnikovism, thought Lenin, could serve as a bargaining chip to offer the Western powers in return for trade, credits, recognition, and repudiation of pre-war debts.

But the Genoa conference failed. Instead of a general détente with the Western powers, the Soviets instead shifted into a bloc of the pariahs when it signed the Treaty of Rapallo with Germany. Rapallo signaled a policy of dogged opposition to the Treaty of Versailles, which the Bolsheviks had been cultivating with the German army since 1920. Lenin suffered his first stroke while this turn was being affected. As he convalesced and studied the new situation, he gradually dropped his support for Sokolnikov and came over to the views of Trotsky. By October 1922, he and Trotsky had formed a bloc to save the monopoly of foreign trade, to protect and subsidize industry, and to support the GOSPLAN against those who called it a "nest of the spetsy."

At the same time Zinoviev, Kamenev, and Stalin drew increasingly closer. In the party ranks it was assumed that Zinoviev was the leader of the bloc. Party workers noted that the leaders were listed alphabetically (according to the Russian alphabet) but they also thought they were listed in order of importance. Here was the head of the Leningrad apparatus and the Communist International (Zinoviev), the head of the Moscow party apparatus (Kamenev), and the head of the Workers and Peasants Inspectorate (*rabkrin*), the party's Central Control Commission, and the General Secretariat (Stalin). In view of Lenin's illness, it seemed that this would be the collective leadership to succeed Lenin if the worst were to come to pass. The grouping of Zinoviev-Kamenev-Stalin had originated in the "Lenin faction" during the trade union debate. They were well used to fighting Trotsky with Lenin's subtle encouragement, but now they were also fighting Lenin. Stalin, who was assigned the supervision of Lenin's doctors, was not frightened by this, especially in view of the two further strokes that Lenin suffered in December. Stalin judged, in his own delicate way, that "Lenin ist kaput." It was unfair to say that he did not know foreign languages.

The bloc of Lenin and Trotsky was shaping up when, after a series of clashes with Stalin over rudeness in some personal matters, Lenin dictated a series of letters comprising his "testament." These documents have been interpreted variously, although they seem straightforward enough. In assessing the leaders of the party, Lenin suggested (he was alone in this) that Stalin and Trotsky were much weightier than anyone else in the leadership. Stalin was worrisome because of his power and Trotsky because of his brilliance and arrogance. Lenin wanted collective leadership to continue, but he thought the biggest problem was that Stalin and Trotsky would split the party, so he urged the members of the party to limit them both. In an addendum, he rethought his original notes and concluded that Stalin, because of his being so *nekulturnyi*, was the greater problem, which the party should solve by removing him from his position as General Secretary and in effect "crushing Stalin politically," as one of his personal secretaries later characterized his position. To this end Lenin wanted Trotsky to present an anti-Stalin "platform" to the Twelfth Party Congress in the spring of 1923.

This was the rub. There was no real case against Stalin, only, as in Lenin's vague anti-Trotsky line of 1920, some dim forebodings about bureaucracy—the abuses in the *rabkrin*, and in the Control Commission, and Stalin's having been rude to some Georgian comrades. Not much of a platform. It is not surprising that Trotsky failed to take it up at the Congress. When Bukharin made some mention of it, he was ignored. The point was that neither Trotsky nor Bukharin could take on Stalin and the "Lenin faction" without Lenin at their side. And only Lenin himself could have done it without a burning issue to serve as rationale. Most Bolsheviks would have thought that, if the issue was important, any regime would be appropriate. They would have cited the civil war. When one wills the end, one wills the means. Only Lenin would even have thought to base opposition to a given leader on the "regime question," the threat of overweening power. Those who have depicted Lenin as the demiurge of the purest form of Totalitarianism should at least consider this.

It is by no means sure that Trotsky thought Stalin important enough to worry about. Zinoviev was his keenest and most entrenched opponent and was already preparing a kind of theoretical case against "Trotskyism" in an outline history of Bolshevism in which Trotsky's 1905 slogan, "No Tsar but a Workers State," was contrasted to the views of Lenin. In the fall of 1923 a group of prominent Bolsheviks who had been excluded from key positions by the personnel changes since the tenth congress made a protest against bureaucracy in the form of a Platform of the Forty-Six. A major party controversy loomed up in Russia.

This happened at the same time as a revolutionary change in Germany, where a general strike had caused the Communists there to prepare a bid for power. The Comintern had been showing a veiled sympathy for the German policy of currency inflation as a way of contending with their requirement to pay war reparations. It saw this as a kind of revolt by the Germans against their semi-colonial status under the Entente, that is, under the French. The German Communist leaders grouped around Heinrich Brandler had been installed by Moscow in 1921, largely through the agency of Karl Radek, the Comintern's leading man on German problems. They dutifully tried to balance criticism of their government with denunciation of its enemies, the Entente imperialists who, they said, sought to enslave Germany. When the French drew the conclusion that the Germans were deliberately delaying their payments in kind, they sent French troops into the Rhineland. The Germans, under the Cuno government, escalated their inflation of the mark to the point of hyperinflation. German currency became almost worthless. But a general strike brought down the German government in August 1923, replacing its leader Cuno with Gustav Stresemann, who pledged to end the inflation and patch things up with the French. Thus Moscow had two reasons, a Comintern reason and a foreign policy reason, to try to overthrow Stresemann.

In the end Trotsky did not sign the Platform of the Forty-Six, although he said later that it had been the beginning of the struggle against the Thermidorean bureaucracy led by Stalin. At the time he said no such thing. He only responded in a separate letter with his own vague complaints but did not mention Stalin. In 1926, he admitted that he had at the time judged the center of apparatus bureaucratism to be in Leningrad, that is, in Zinoviev's machine. This admission makes more sense than historical accounts that assume a Trotsky-Stalin struggle in 1923.

At any rate, the Russian crisis passed and the German October failed. The German Communists did not get the aid they expected from the provincial Social Democrats, and the uprising ended in a fiasco. It was a terrible defeat. The Bolsheviks had lived for the German revolution, the only event that could in the end justify their having taken power in Russia. There was no dissent on this; the Russian revolution could only make sense as a trigger for the world revolution. As Marxists, they could never have entertained the idea of modernizing Russia by themselves. And now the German revolution had failed. The Russian Communist idea was refuted. Perhaps they should have said, "Sorry, but we no longer have a reason for being. We will resign and leave Russia to its devices." But people are not like that. They tried instead to say something different, that the revolution was experiencing temporary difficulties and that its contact with reality would be resumed shortly. It took some faith to say this. On the other hand, no one could deny that they did have control of a powerful state, as the Italian Socialist Angelo Tasca had said, "not a country but a continent." Perhaps they could find a way to manage.

At first they thought that the problem was not what to do next, but how to assign the blame. Lenin's death in January 1924 made this urgent from the standpoint of the succession. At a meeting of the Comintern executive, Ruth Fischer, speaking for the left wing "Berlin opposition" in the German Communist party, offered a perversely ingenious explanation for the failure of the German October. It was, she said, the fault of the policy of Heinrich Brandler, the head of the German party. Instead of preparing for the revolution, Brandler had been coquetting with a "National Bolshevik" line of tacit support for the Cuno government's campaign against the French: too much diplomacy and not enough revolutionism. But Brandler's policy came from Moscow, and he had been installed in the German leadership by the Russian Bolshevik Karl Radek. To whom was Radek closest in Moscow? Trotsky, the real author of the National Bolshevik line in Germany! "Trotskyism," which had cropped up in the Soviet Union, had a branch in Germany in the Brandler leadership. It was international "Trotskyism" that had failed the German revolution.

Zinoviev's eyes lit up. As head of the Comintern he was on the spot. He would have been the logical one to assume at least some responsibility for the debacle, but this argument offered a way out and served his purposes in the succession struggle as well. Zinoviev resolved to crush "Trotskyism" in Russia and in the Comintern. But what did this mean? Was there such a thing? In the summer of 1924, at the fifth congress of the Comintern, Zinoviev managed to remove the leaders of the French and German parties as Trotskyites. Those who were purged complained in their own defense that there was no "Trotskyism." Zinoviev replied that Trotskyism in the Comintern was softness toward the Social Democrats, who were in his view actually "social fascists," the left wing of the fascist movement. There must be a Bolshevization of the Comintern, a campaign for "Integral Leninism," "Marxism-Leninism," "100% Leninism." Zinoviev conjured up a broad "democratic" Leninism against a "narrow" proletarian Trotskyism. In his telling, Trotskyism was everything Trotsky did before 1917, such as opposing Lenin's old slogan of the Democratic Dictatorship of the Proletariat and the Peasantry with the idea of Permanent Revolution. This showed that Trotsky was "hostile to the peasant." Real Marxist-Leninists must make a turn: "Face to the Countryside"! In Comintern affairs as well, it was time for a Peasant International to be formed alongside the Communists, time for American Communists to help the movement for a Farmer-Labor party.

At the Thirteenth Party Congress, a Lenin Levy of 240,000 new members was brought into the party. Stalin got an iron grip on the Soviet Communist party while Zinoviev got control of the Comintern. The Testament was read to the Politburo but not to the Congress. Trotsky decided to keep his silence, lest it be thought that he defended "Trotskyism," which he said pertained only to the period before 1917 and was something only for the archives. But in the fall, in the introduction to an edition of his collected works, titled *Lessons of October*, he attacked Zinoviev and Kamenev (but not Stalin), saying that the two "strikebreakers of October" had also bungled the German revolution. This cruel retort kindled a two-month campaign, in which virtually all the leading lights of Communism in Russia and abroad weighed in against "Trotskyism." The *Lessons of October* conjured up an image of the revolution pitted against the party. Stalin claimed that Trotsky and the Military Revolutionary Committee of the Petrograd Soviet had not led the October insurrection, as he had freely admitted hitherto. Instead, he said, it was done by a party organization with him at the lead, one that did not include Trotsky. In the telling of history at least, Stalin strove to assert the party's superiority over the revolution itself.

Countless pamphlets and circulars were published, in all the languages of the Comintern parties, considering "Leninism or Trotskyism?" Accusations were in all colors of the rainbow and were limited only by the imaginations of the critics. They tended to center on accusations of Trotsky's presumed "Bonapartism." This sort of campaign could not have occurred while Lenin was alive. He never propounded "Marxism-Leninism" and would probably not have tolerated it. Finally, to defuse the attacks, Trotsky resigned his post as Commissar of War. This occasion used to be cited in some historical accounts as an opportunity for a military coup, but Trotsky did not control the commissar apparatus, nor did he suppose such a thing to be thinkable in any event. Even so, it was probably his decisive defeat.

No sooner did Trotsky step down than Stalin broke with Zinoviev. In an essay called "The October Revolution and the Tactics of the Russian Communists," he made a new departure. He said that Trotsky had been wrong to suppose that the Soviets could only be saved by "state support" from Europe, that is, by a revolution in an advanced country. The existence of the regime owed much, he claimed, to "moral support" rendered by opposition of workers in the West to their governments' anti-Soviet plans. Socialism in One Country need not be doomed if it received this continued moral support. In Stalin's exposition foreign Communists had a key role as fifth columns for

Soviet national interest. Ostensibly directed against Trotsky, this notion cut directly against Zinoviev. Moreover, Stalin came to the aid of Trotsky against Zinoviev. He said that Zinoviev had erred in calling Trotsky a Menshevik and urging his ouster from the party. Trotsky's was only a less dangerous species of "right Bolshevism." Thus Stalin's introduction of Socialism in One Country marked both a break with Zinoviev and reconciliation with Trotsky.

No sooner was Stalin's break with Zinoviev perceived than Bukharin loomed up in the latter's place, defending Socialism in One Country as the purest "Marxism-Leninism," just as Sokolnikov had done earlier with Lenin's state capitalism. Bukharin opposed Zinoviev's excesses in Comintern policy and accused him of hostility to NEP. A Stalin-Bukharin bloc with a rightist policy took center stage in 1925–1926. Bukharin's ally Tomsky set up an Anglo-Russian Joint Action Committee linking the Soviet and British trade unions to serve as the centerpiece of the policy of "moral support" from the western workers. Trotsky sat through all this without comment, trying to live down his "Trotskyism." It was Zinoviev who went on the attack. He called the Stalin-Bukharin policy "Mensheviko-Ustrialovism." The kulak, the NEPman, and the bureaucrat were the beneficiaries of the right's line. In 1926, he called it a "Thermidorean" tendency. He aimed his primary fire against Bukharin rather than Stalin. Stalin made occasional disavowals of the extremes of Bukharin's line to keep a centrist position.

The Fourteenth Party Congress at the end of 1925 saw a showdown between Zinoviev and the Leningrad apparatus and Bukharin's Moscow supporters. The Leningraders were soundly beaten. Stalin rose up to defend Bukharin and Trotsky against them. The Politburo was shaken up and weighted more heavily in favor of supporters of Stalin-Bukharin. Zinoviev lost the Leningrad organization to Sergei Kirov. Kamenev lost his Politburo seat. The full members were now Stalin, Trotsky, Zinoviev, Bukharin, Rykov, Tomsky, Kalinin, to whom were added Molotov and Voroshilov. These changes were thought at the time to be gains for the Stalin-Bukharin bloc, but several members turned out later to be simply supporters of Stalin. Some began to perceive that Stalin was not merely the executor of Bukharin's brilliant theoretical formulations, but a real force in his own rite. Some perceived this, but not many.

Trotsky was happy to see the Leningraders defeated. This did not occur to Western observers and to many later students of the subject, who wondered why Trotsky did not throw his support behind Zinoviev against Stalin. Trotsky later revealed that, if he had entered the fray, it would have been on the side of Stalin and Bukharin. Afterward, however, Trotsky did approach Bukharin for a joint campaign simply to get the regime to ease up, especially in the matter of anti-Semitic attacks made against him by Bukharin's ally, Uglanov, head of the Moscow apparat. But Bukharin did not bite.

Trotsky now saw that a career of toadying to the duumvirs loomed ahead for him. In April 1926 he took the extraordinary step of talking to Zinoviev about a bloc, at first on the economic policy of the right. After the failure of the British general strike in May 1926 they both said for the first time that Tomsky's strategy of cooperation with the British trade unions was a failure and a betrayal of British Communism. Gradually they added a criticism of Comintern policy on China where the Communists were running aground, as we will see in the next chapter. These three issues, economic policy, the British general strike, and the Chinese revolution, united the joint opposition of Zinoviev and Trotsky.

The showdown came in 1927, after the British raided the Arcos trading mission in London and, claiming evidence of subversion, broke off diplomatic relations with Soviet Russia. In Moscow this was feared as a prelude to an invasion of the Soviet Union. There was a war scare in the press, each side in the party struggle accusing the other of not being prepared to defend the country. Trotsky allowed himself to be baited into a comparison of his situation with that of the French leader Clemenceau, during the war, who had offered himself as alternative leadership to save the nation. Trotsky accepted the analogy in what his enemies took to calling his "Clemenceau statement." Ten years later, scores of old Bolsheviks would be tried and shot for taking part in a vast conspiracy that began, it was charged, with the "Clemenceau statement."

The war scare lasted into the fall and reached a climax at the ceremonies on the tenth anniversary of the revolution. The opposition made a public demonstration in the two capitals, but nothing much resulted from it. Afterward, Zinoviev and Kamenev capitulated and confessed their error of falling into Trotskyism. It was the first of many confessions. "To get to the helm," said Zinoviev, "we must pay the price." Trotsky noted ironically that they had indeed paid the price, but the helm was nowhere in sight.

At the Fifteenth Party Congress, December 1927, Trotsky and the opposition were expelled from the party. A month later Trotsky was deported to Alma Ata in Soviet Turkestan. Within a year he would be expelled from the Soviet Union. By that time Stalin had already emancipated himself from Bukharin by initiating the fateful turn toward the collectivization of agriculture. Stalin had started out on the left with Zinoviev against Trotsky, then gone to the right with Bukharin against Zinoviev, now back left with Zinoviev against Bukharin. Each turn lifted his stature and powers against the others. The centrist position had shown Stalin the right path to power. It could do so only in an atmosphere where other "Leninists" opposed each other more than they opposed Stalin and only on the condition of their underestimating him. That was why only Stalin, and not a more brilliant fellow, could play the centrist role to perfection. He seemed to have got to the top, but greater heights still beckoned. More abrupt turns were still to come.

CHAPTER 8

National Bolshevism in World Affairs

The Russian Bolsheviks started out with the intention to over-throw the existing cosmos, not merely to liberate or modernize Russia. They thought of themselves as the only remaining internationalists in a world that had drunkenly served up all its values on the altar of war. That was supposed to give them a special and superior perspective from which to look down on the cruel world of international relations. From the beginning they knew that defeatism was a cause that might not triumph everywhere simultaneously, so one had to recognize that the defeat of Russia would also be the victory of its enemies. But they laughed off the denunciations hurled at them in Petrograd for the help they had got from Ludendorff. When Germany rose up in revolution they could join it in common cause against the Entente imperialists. A Communist Germany would thus have resulted in a German-Russian heartland bloc, the nightmare of Sir Halford Mackinder, the British authority on the new science of geopolitics. Mackinder had warned that the power controlling the heartland of the Eurasian land mass would control the world. Communists could not deny that an expanded socialist commonwealth might take the *form* of a Bismarckian or Metternichean bloc in Central and Eastern Europe. But they were sure that its *content* would be pro-letarian socialism of the purest kind and a rebuke to imperialism, the balance of power, and the idea of the nation-state itself.

There is no good reason to doubt their sincerity about this. It was entirely natural for them to consider themselves the most militant voice in a general chorus of disillusionment with the "old diplomacy" that had brought on the horrors of the war. Like many liberals and pacifists they wanted to transcend war and patriotism in the name of a new idealistic world order. But what if these plans should falter? What if they should be forced to retreat into the perspective of a single country? What should one country's attitude toward world politics be? Many Western liberals and pacifists never succeeded in answering this question about their own countries prior to the outbreak of a second war in 1939. In any case, Communists never had any difficulty choosing to defend Soviet Russia. They did not renounce their original revolutionary euphoria but made it rhyme with Soviet foreign policy.

In some ways the revolution reinforced the traditional Russian foreign policy. Tsarist Russia had always pressed on the Straits, Central Asia, and the Far East, to the consternation of the British, who were obsessed with the fear of a Russian advance on India. Revolutionary Russia sent what the British thought to be dangerous anti-imperialist propaganda in the same direction. There was no denying that this was a reversal of the position of nineteenth-century Marxism. To be sure, Marx and Engels had pointed out the various hypocrisies of the European imperialists and had sympathized with India, but nowhere in their writings could one find a perspective of the colonial world rising up and overthrowing its imperial masters, still less of Russia as a progressive force *vis-à-vis* Britain. Yet the Bolsheviks now urged all the colonies to throw off the European yoke. For a few months in 1918–1919, when things looked dark outside of a shrinking red bastion in central Russia, Trotsky had even speculated about the road to Beijing or Singapore being shorter than that to Paris or London. There was no Marxist precedent for views like these.

If Bolshevism was the ally of the subject colonial world against Western imperialism, that made the British and French the first enemies of Communism. Communists thus had to consider Britain and France incomparably more odious than Germany, who had lost her small colonial empire in Africa and now lay under the heel of the Entente. It followed that Communism must be the support of the defeated countries most likely to have national revolutions against the Entente. The Hungarian Soviet Republic of 1919 was the first experiment in national Communism. This was immediately followed by the agitation in a Communist cell in Hamburg for what was called "National Bolshevism," according to which Germany in defeat had been "proletarianized" and required, not a counterrevolutionary civil war, but a national rising in league with Soviet Russia. The Hamburg Communists authored a pamphlet with the title "Revolutionärer Volkskrieg oder Konterrevolutionärer Bürgerkrieg?" (Revolutionary Peoples' War or Counter-Revolutionary Civil War?). Even under the

Kaiser, they said, Germany had led a world movement against the British Empire. Eventually the Soviet expert on German affairs, Karl Radek, would be preaching a variant of this line to German generals: the Entente (Britain and France) holds your country in slavery; only a proletarian revolution can restore its military greatness.

There were echoes of these ideas all over Europe. Even Mussolini, on his way to the creation of fascism, went through a "National Bolshevik" phase in 1919, advocating that Italy make common cause with the "proletarian" nations, among whom he counted Russia, Germany, Hungary, and Bulgaria. These were, he judged, much better than Italy's miserable Entente allies. In a similar, anti-Entente spirit, the Comintern declared that France was incapable of organizing Europe and only capable of "balkanizing" it. This, it was said, had been her reason for waging war. On the other hand, Communist revolution would build a Workers' and Peasants' Europe. Trotsky envisioned revival of his old idea of a Socialist United States of Europe, a fortress capable of withstanding blockade by England and America. While the Kaiser was certainly no socialist, prior to the war he had also called for a United States of Europe against the Anglo-Saxons.

These were the notions with which the Comintern went into the German revolution of October 1923. They called Germany a country oppressed by colonialism in the same way as India. Soviet propaganda in favor of revisionist nations who sought to change the European peace settlement dovetailed nicely with anti-imperial propaganda in the third world. Radek confidently predicted that National Bolshevism would win the entire east for Communism. He was thinking of the prospects for anti-colonial revolutionary movements. Soviet foreign policy also moved the process along by coming to the aid of the two pre-war "sick men" who had seemed likely at the turn of the century to be candidates for partition: Turkey and China.

Some Soviet Bolsheviks went too far. Mir Said Sultan-Galiev, a Tatar Communist from Kazan, argued for national Communism in Turkestan, Azerbaijan, Tataria, and Bashkiria. He also sought their liberation from Russia. He called them "proletarian nations" like those in the third world. He said that Communism would triumph first in Asia. The Bolsheviks quickly suppressed Sultan Galiev's agitation, but Lenin may have been affected by similar thoughts, to the degree of harboring sympathy for all who resented Great Russian chauvinism. He got his way over Stalin, then Commissar of Nationalities, who wanted to include the non-Russian peoples in a Russian federation. Instead they became part of the Union of Soviet Socialist Republics in 1922.

The Soviets helped nationalist Turkey to defend itself against Britain in 1920–1922. Greek troops with British backing invaded Anatolia and came up against Turkish resistance led by Mustapha Kemal, which managed to drive the Greeks back to the Aegean coast. The Soviets, after settling the Armenian border with Kemal, lent him arms and other support against the Greeks and British. For his part, Kemal proclaimed the gratitude of the Turkish people to the revolutionary workers and peasants of Soviet Russia, and the solidarity of all against imperialism. As for Turkish Communists, however, they were subjected to harshest repression. This was to become a pattern in relations between Soviet Russia and anti-imperialist nationalists.

The Soviets tried to make use of the Pan-Turk and Islamist sentiment in Central Asia to spread the revolt against British Imperialism. In the words of Sultan-Galiev: "Just as Soviet Turkestan was the revolutionary beacon for Chinese Turkestan, Afghanistan, Tibet, India, Bukhara, and Khiva, so will Soviet Azerbaijan be the beacon for Persia, Arabia, and Turkey." Kuchik Khan, a bandit warlord in northern Persia, helped local Communists to set up a Ghilan Republic in Persian Azerbaijan. But, when the Soviets signed the Anglo-Soviet trade treaty in March 1921, they agreed to abandon him. Reza Khan, a soldier set up as head of the Persian state by the British, routed Kuchik Khan. However, even after defeating the Ghilan republic, Reza Shah (he would overthrow the Qajar Shah in 1925) did not want to be a British puppet. He signed a treaty with the Soviets and subordinated the British. He acted very much like Kemal.

Amanullah Khan seized power in Afghanistan in February 1919. He preached the jihad against imperialism in league with the Soviets, who made him independent of the British by sending him arms and planes. He attacked India in May. When the British bombed Kabul and Jalalabad, he relented. He continued to look to central and southern Asia to build an Islamic federation, especially to the Basmachi revolt against the Soviets in the Fergana valley, which smoldered on for years. His ideas seemed to cut against imperialism and Communism to the same degree. The Soviets tried to maintain a Communist Bureau in Tashkent dispensing propaganda into India. They supported the Khilifat movement of Indian Muslims seeking to restore the Caliphate. The Bureau continued to annoy the British until they issued an ultimatum to the Soviets in 1923: close it or lose the trade treaty. That was its end.

The Soviets directed serious efforts to aid revolution in China. When the Treaty of Versailles recognized the Japanese interests in China, there was a nationalist revolt. The May 4th Movement simultaneously launched the Chinese Communist party and the nationalist

Kuomintang, both fiercely anti-Japanese and anti-British. In 1922–1923, the Washington Naval Treaty and the Four Power Pact guaranteeing Chinese territorial integrity were taken as a cover for a foreign conspiracy to establish the Open Door in China. The Soviets encouraged the Communists to join the Kuomintang and fight to unify the country. They would support the great northern march in 1926–1927 up to the point when General Chiang Kai-chek turned on them in May 1927.

In general, National Bolshevism seemed at first to work well against the British Empire. The Bolsheviks had no trouble making use of "Kemalism" in campaigns to give several countries more leverage against Britain. At the same time this did not prevent the same countries from persecuting their own Communist parties. Later in the 1920s countries with which the Soviets had been intimate turned to a policy of equidistance between them and Britain, and after that to a policy of anti-Soviet hostility. For the moment, at least, the road to Paris did not run through Asia.

Foreign Communists seemed to change their line with every hint from Moscow, but they were not at first merely an instrument of Soviet foreign policy. They pursued the idea of world revolution. At the same time, the International could not be sure how to describe the emerging ideology of Communism or how to apply criteria for admission. A Communist had to be someone who was against the war, against imperialism, and for the Russian revolution. He also had to believe that the Social Democracy was opportunist and that this had somehow caused its betrayal of internationalism in 1914. Lenin and Trotsky said this while, in fact, they knew they had no prewar record of opposition to Social Democratic opportunism. Bolshevism had never been a separate international trend. Bolsheviks and "Trotskyists" had rigorously followed the dictates of the Socialist International, which meant that they were in the intellectual tutelage of the German socialists.

After the war and the revolution Lenin railed against Karl Kautsky and his "social patriotism." Kautsky had been the leading theoretical voice of German Social Democracy in the prewar years. He came around to the position of supporting the German government in the war, for which he earned Lenin's sobriquet, "renegade" Kautsky. But prior to the war Lenin never gave the slightest suggestion of distrust of Kautsky and the Germans, and even challenged others who mistakenly assumed something of the kind to name one instance where he had ever criticized Kautsky's opportunism. His world was shattered in August 1914 when he learned of the German Social Democrats' vote for war credits. Lenin afterward ransacked history for a retrospective suggestion of their treachery, but could only muster a claim that they had dropped reference to the Dictatorship of the Proletariat and misinterpreted Marx's writings on the Paris Commune. That was the only evidence he could adduce of the opportunism that would lead the workers into war in 1914. In fact, he never solved this problem, and Soviet historiography groaned under it as long as the Communist regime was in existence.

Only anarchists had a record of criticism of the German Social Democracy. Lenin admitted in an unguarded moment that they had correctly analyzed the worst features of opportunism. In this sense, Communism was more the heir of nineteenth-century anarchism than of Marxist Social Democracy. Many of the new Communists in Russia and Europe had been anarchists or syndicalists. They were usually enthusiasts of "mass action" or "council communism." This was fine if one remembered the unity of Bolsheviks and anarchists in Petrograd in 1917 and if the revolution they preached were truly on the morrow. But suppose it was not? What could they do in a non-revolutionary time? By the Third Comintern Congress in 1921, Lenin and Trotsky had recovered their social democratic reflexes enough to realize that there was no alternative to peaceful parliamentary and trade union activity. Revolutionaries would now have to do work that was hardly distinguishable from what social democrats normally do. Communist parties could not make this turn toward work in a united front with Social Democrats and British Labourites without internal splits and frictions. The Communist International represented as fragile and temporary an alliance of moods as that of 1917.

This would not have troubled any of the Communist leaders who sensed that Europe would be aflame with revolution within two or three years. But suppose the revolution was tardy? Then new tactics would have to be devised, tactics that would have to be made compatible with the interests of the Soviet state. The problem became palpable after the March Action of 1921, in which Communists, preaching the "offensive," tried and failed miserably to propel the German workers into insurrection. The German military was reassured by this puny showing that they had nothing to fear from the revolution. The result was that they threw themselves even more willingly into their clandestine cooperation with the Red Army to thwart the Versailles peace. German business pressed for better trade relations. Oddly, it seemed that failure of the German revolution only cemented Soviet-German relations.

Eventually this reality had to affect the Comintern. Paul Levi, who led the German Communists, had called the March Action "the greatest Bakuninist putsch in history." Levi did not think much of Bukharin's theory of "the offensive," nor of the agitation of Comintern agents in Germany. He thought that Communists would have to settle down and act more like social democrats. His open denunciation of the "offensive" infuriated Lenin and caused him to press for Levi's expulsion. In dismissing him, however, Lenin was careful to take his advice. Levi had argued for a united front with the hated Social Democrats and for parliamentary agitation for a pact between Germany and Soviet Russia. His ideas became the policy of the German Communists, pursued more or less faithfully for the next decade. They implied opposition to the British and especially to the French and, one way or another, support, or at least parallel action, with any German government set on defying the West. It was natural for the Comintern economist Eugen Varga to express sympathy for Germany as an "industrial colony" of the imperialists. There were instances of conflict between Comintern and Soviet foreign policy, to be sure. Soviet diplomats often cringed at the sound of Communist propaganda. Yet, as long as these larger perspectives were kept in mind, there was no real contradiction between Comintern and Soviet foreign policy.

Yet the question remained: When would the Soviet Union break out of its isolation? At the Twentieth Comintern Congress in 1920, G. M. Serrati, for the Italian Socialists, had suggested that Communism could not take any detours away from Europe. It would either expand there or, one day, either the Soviet experiment would collapse from within or the forces of world reaction would destroy it from without. To many European Socialists this was a perfectly sound Marxist prognostication. Why did it prove to be so wrong?

CHAPTER 9

Collectivization of Agriculture and Five-Year Plan, 1929–1933

I n 1928 the party, led by Stalin and his Politburo group, took the fateful step of abandoning the NEP and initiating the collectivization of agriculture, to be accompanied by the adoption of a five-year plan, the first of many. In the view of the Stalin leadership, socialism and planned economy were no longer prohibited by the economic conditions prevailing in a predominantly peasant country. Possessing the state power, Stalin resolved to use it to industrialize the nation at the expense of peasant.

One can say that this was always the implicit intention of the most radical voices in the party, especially the left critics of the Stalin-Bukharin bloc, although most of them shrunk from the prospect. One could also say that Lenin himself, who had urged cooperation with the peasants, also feared that small proprietorship impinged on the proletarian dictatorship in small ways, persistently and in increasing proportions. Stalin was himself probably looking for a way to force things into a large-scale campaign that he could lead to get free of the Bukharin group and to eclipse the others with whom he had been forced to work as an equal in the collective leadership. The decisions were already indicated in 1927 but the leap into the abyss was forced in January 1928 when it was discovered that grain deliveries were two million tons short of that thought to be necessary to feed the workers in the cities. The peasants had staged a "grain strike."

The Great Turn was the last link in a chain of events in which the Russian revolution came up against international resistance in its attempt to kindle a world revolution. The chain might extend back as far as the British general strike of 1926, which prompted calls in the British parliament for a "counteroffensive" against the Russian revolution, which led to the British compromise with the Chinese Kuomintang, which led to the Kuomintang's defeat of the Chinese Communists, all of which moved the British to break relations with the Soviet Union, which led to the war scare of 1927, which frightened the Russian peasants into withholding grain from the cities in the "grain strike" of January 1928, which prompted the emergency measures to "take grain," which turned into the Great Turn.

Economic issues had not been the sole matter of contention, nor even the center of the debate in the party, during the tangled succession struggle that had permitted Stalin to rise to supreme power. At first disputes revolved around historical and ideological issues. "Leninism" was invented by invoking its antonym, "Trotskyism." Then the debate shifted to Comintern policy: Who was responsible for the failure of the German revolution and the isolation of the Soviet state? Once isolation had been accepted by all, at least as a possible condition for the next significant interval, economic policy became increasingly important. Bukharin's line on the economy rose to prominence in 1924–1925 and Zinoviev opposed it, calling it "Mensheviko-Ustrialovism."

It seemed to follow that Zinoviev should offer an economic program as an alternative. But this took shape in a confused way. Trotsky did not join Zinoviev in opposition until 1926, and when he did, economic policy was one of the first areas of agreement between the old enemies. Neither of them wanted to revisit Trotsky's ideas of the Trade Union Debate of 1920, with the "militarization of labor" slogan. Trotsky had said many other left things during the civil war, calling for "primitive socialist accumulation" and in 1923 speaking vaguely about a socialist offensive within the NEP. But Trotsky could not have been Zinoviev's economist in 1925, when the latter warned of a Thermidorean degeneration in the revolution and accused the Stalin-Bukharin leadership of yielding to the kulak, the NEPman, and the bureaucrat. He was on record espousing an economic line advocating a kind of Sokolnikovist promotion of interdependence with the gold standard countries, a view that was perfectly consonant with Bukharin's. More to the point, Trotsky was not in opposition.

When Zinoviev put out a call for all the prior oppositions to group under his wing, economist Evgenii Preobrazhenskii, one of the Forty-Six in 1923, answered it. He began to take up the argument against Bukharin's economic policy. By 1927, the Left Opposition was to include not only Trotsky and Preobrazhenskii but also the former Finance Minister Sokolnikov, who had argued in 1922 for "state capitalism." This allowed Bukharin and Stalin to have their fun alluding to the economic confusion in the opposition's ranks.

Preobrazhenskii's arguments were the most striking and original. He held that if the Soviet state were to remain isolated it would have no choice but to take up primitive socialist accumulation with a vengeance. He referred the comrades to the last chapters of Marx's *Capital* with their lurid description of primary accumulation, the worldwide process that, in Marx's reading, took many guises in different historical settings, enclosure of the common lands in England, slavery in Africa and the Americas, the dispossession of the indigenous tribes in the American West. All of this was part of the process of separating the agriculturalist from his land and delivering him to the city to build industry. "And the history of this, their expropriation," Marx intoned, "is written in the annals of mankind in letters of blood and fire." A horrible process carried out by the bourgeoisie. The Communist was only expected to appear much later, after the bourgeoisie was historically superseded by the proletariat.

However, Preobrazhenskii was now saying that the Communists were going to have to carry out primary accumulation in Russia— and in a short period of time. The Russian revolution could not lean on the industry of a socialist Germany, nor could it lure foreign investment from the capitalist world. Industrialization must in the end be paid for by the Russian peasant alone and, since he was not likely to do it voluntarily, he must be coerced by the Communists. They must force him to provide food at prices favorable to the city; they must force him to provide recruits for city industry; they must force him to save. That is, he must learn to live on less. He was not to be starved but put on a severe diet.

Stalin read Preobrazhenskii with avid interest. He had long admired the book that the economist had written with Bukharin in 1920, the *ABC of Communism*, a book in which War Communism was not treated as an temporary expedient but as a method for the introduction of socialism under revolutionary conditions. Another economist, S. G. Strumilin, wrote an article that impressed Stalin, speaking of the need to treat the economy as something that could not only be studied but also changed by a party armed with the state power and capable of dictating the tempo.

This was such a daunting prospect that none of the other prominent figures, Trotsky included, could bring themselves to endorse it. Yet it was to be the way Stalin's Soviet Union would take its characteristic shape in the next decade. Trotsky had argued in 1923 that the "scissors" (the gap between food and raw material prices on the one hand,

and prices of manufactured goods on the other) must be closed. That was a line designed to preserve the *smychka*, the union between city and countryside. If the question "Who pays for the NEP?" were asked, Trotsky's answer would have been "the worker." This view, which Trotsky held from 1923 to 1926, was not fundamentally opposed to Bukharin's. For his part, Bukharin had reacted to the charge that he favored the peasant (see Chapter 7) by a moderate limitation of the NEP in 1926–1927. He and Stalin made some rural transactions illegal and subjected others to a superprofits tax. The private sector's share of the national income actually shrunk by about 7 percent, and the NEPman's share of the total trade similarly. These measures did not make the peasants more eager to sell to the city, in view of the paucity of urban products, the "goods famine."

If things were far from ideal with economic policy, they were worse with Comintern policy. Tomsky's maneuvers and the general strike had only driven the British more firmly into the arms of the Diehards, the right wing of the Conservative party, who were calling for an end to the trade treaty and a counteroffensive against world Communism. For the Kremlin, China policy was a disaster. The Zinoviev-Trotsky opposition had tied the economic and Comintern issues into a package with its Platform of 1927. In response, by the end of summer, Stalin resolved to make a turn, a repudiation of everything that he and Bukharin had stood for during the last three years. Stalin had risen to the top through moderate policies associated with Bukharin's name. They were the center of gravity of the NEP, from which he now contemplated a break.

Signs of the Great Turn were visible first in Comintern policy with Mao Tse-tung's Autumn Harvest Rising in August. It seemed a break with the pro-Kuomintang line. The Soviet party also resolved on a turn toward industry, the dimensions of which were not immediately apparent. Then, at the Fifteenth Congress in December, Trotsky was expelled and the party got news of the Canton Commune, a rising of Communists put down by the Kuomintang. It appeared to be a general turn to the left. Once Trotsky had been driven out of the party, a fresh crisis and opportunity was presented to Stalin by the the "grain strike." The prospect of workers, many of them ex-peasants, fleeing the cities to come back to the village and get closer to the source of food filled the party with dread. Why had the peasants withheld grain? Perhaps because of the increasing limits on their economic activity having reached a critical point; perhaps because the scissors were opening; perhaps because of the goods famine; perhaps because of the war scare.

Politically Stalin was in a tight spot. The Left opposition had turned out to be right on a number of issues, or so many might think. Should he yield to them or simply steal their program and give it a redoubled vehemence? Should he try an escape forward and the collectivization of agriculture by force? Stalin decided to answer the grain emergency with his own "emergency measures," sending troops and police to take the grain by military and administrative means. It was an abrupt end to the NEP. Bukharin and his associates were left in the cold. They stayed on in the Politburo while the military campaigns raged on the countryside, arguing against the new line in tense meetings, even achieving a certain correction in summer 1928, which was quickly undone in the fall. The effect was that peasants were herded into collective farms that did not yet exist, then enjoined to build them, then told that things had gone too far, then permitted to flee the "farms," only to be herded back a few months later.

Communists had been told that extreme leftism of this sort was the essence of Trotskyism. They had to learn that the party must be capable of making turns and that it is un-dialectical to stand on principle for any particular political line. Many of them had to be purged to obtain cadres of the requisite hardness and obedience. Collectivization thus forced extensive changes in Stalin's apparatus. New Stalin men came forward to replace the old ones. It was discovered that many who were once thought to be real Communists were merely Bukharinists. The point was made that real Communists are not leftists or rightists, in love with this or that policy, but people like Stalin, hard as nails, part of a cadre that could make turns as the situation demanded. Lenin had been capable of such dramatic turns. Stalin was Lenin today!

Stalin said that the collectivization and five-year plan were matters of life and death for the revolution:

To slacken the pace would be to lag behind and those who lag behind are beaten. We don't want to be beaten. No, we don't want to. The history of old Russia was that she was ceaselessly beaten for her backwardness. She was beaten by the Mongol khans; she was beaten by the Turkish beys; she was beaten by the Swedish feudal lords; she was beaten by the Polish-Lithuanian Pans, she was beaten by the Anglo-French imperialists, she was beaten by the Japanese barons. She was beaten by all for her backwardness. For military backwardness, for political backwardness, for industrial backwardness. She was beaten by all because to beat her was profitable and went unpunished.

We are fifty to a hundred years behind the advanced countries. We must make good this lag in ten years. Either we do it or they crush us.

This was an arresting and enduringly powerful statement of Russia's historical consciousness, as the historian Kliuchevskii might have put it. In 2004, when terrorists perpetrated a horrible outrage against schoolchildren in the southern town of Beslan, Vladimir Putin had recourse to these phrases of Stalin, drawing the apparent lesson that it had all happened because Russia was too weak "and the weak are beaten."

Show trials dramatized the struggle against those who allegedly sought with their foreign accomplices to sabotage the vast campaign in agriculture and industry. The Shakhty trial in 1928 centered on presumed wrecking in the coal industry, aided, it was said, by Polish spies and those who thought like Bukharin. In 1930, it was the turn of the "Industrial Party" featuring a presumed Gosplan conspiracy headed by a Professor Ramzin. All the sentences were commuted and Ramzin was returned to his post. Then it was the Mensheviks and the "Toiling Peasant Party" and the British engineers. Stalin let it be known that the country was awash in saboteurs and traitors, as a rule, in the pay of the Entente.

Collectivization at first tried to set 15–18 million middle peasants and 5–8 million poor peasants against two million "kulaks." Soon it found that the middle peasant was not eager to leave his plot to live in a house that had not yet been built. So he became an enemy, too. Stalin called for "the liquidation of the kulaks as a class." In practice that came to mean kulaks and all who think like them. In the first two years, about one half of the farms were collectivized. Another 10 percent were added by 1933, about 60 percent in all. There were huge losses of livestock. Peasants tried desperately to feast on all that they knew they would lose. Cattle and horses were reduced in numbers by one third, hogs by half, sheep and goats by 40 percent. These were losses that were not made good until the 1950s.

Often peasants resisted in a primitive way, but they were no match for troops. Historian Isaac Deutscher has aptly remarked that it was "not a civil war, but a civil massacre." Collectivization began to put in place some of the features of the regime of High Stalinism that would emerge in the period of Great Purges of 1936–1938. As numerous local rebellions of peasants and townsfolk swept the countryside, they were met by troops and by police and party people, who suppressed them with force where necessary, dividing little movements and arresting and shooting various leaders and "wreckers." The police apparatus grew into a mighty force of social control and oppression.

Many of those arrested were put to work on huge projects. One hundred thousand prisoners built the White Sea–Baltic canal. Others built the canal connecting the Volga to the Moskva River. Forced labor was widely used in the mines and forests. By 1940 some 500 labor camps contained perhaps two and a half million prisoners. There was famine in the North Caucasus, the Volga basin, the Ukraine, and Kazakhstan, areas that were the targets of the most intense effects to collectivize. While this was going on, grain was still exported, and housewives were enjoined to turn in their wedding rings, the gold of which was used to pay Russia's foreign debts and maintain her credit, the better to buy machinery and equipment for the new factories.

The tour de force in agriculture was matched by a tour de force in industry. The industrial working class was increased from 9 million to 24 million. The managerial and administrative intelligentsia increased by three times to two million. Millions of managers carried out the plan directing the work of millions of new workers, most of both strata newly drawn from the countryside. New homes, schools, and facilities had to be built in every city. Acclimatization to urban life was controlled by official exhortation to fulfill and over-fulfill quotas, to carry out shock work, to engage in socialist emulation of the achievements of the shock workers. Aleksei Stakhanov, one day in 1935, mined 102 tons of coal, 14 times his quota. Stakhanovites sprung up in every industry and surpassed him. The press showered praise on the heroes of socialist shock work.

Soviet media pointed with pride to the raw achievements in quantities of steel, coal, oil, electricity, machine tools, but also of schools, textbooks, hospitals, libraries, and, more pertinently, tanks, artillery, small arms, and aircraft. The Five Year plan gave the country the Dnieper Power Station, the Stalingrad Tractor Plant, the Rostov Agricultural Machinery works, the Magnitogorsk Metallurgical Combine, the Turkistan-Siberian Railway, and the coal and iron complex of the Kuznets Basin. Massive dams throttled the titanic Russian rivers. Huge semi-gothic skyscrapers rose in the center of big towns as they had in the United States in the 1920s. The entire country was transformed from top to bottom at a time when the Western economies were mired in the great depression and looking with unease at the nightmarish mocking Soviet model, hopefully not an example that would spread.

Was all this necessary? For historians of the Soviet Union, this is the question of questions. Even in the midst of the glasnost campaign of 1987–1989, when Mikhail Gorbachev issued a call for honest historical

reassessments, Soviet academics could not decide about collectivization. A Western school of thought that rose up in the 1970s and 1980s
concluded that it was not necessary. Soviet industry might have been
better served by measures of a more gradual nature that ensured the
supply of food. Soviet historians, cursing their intellectual dilemma,
admitted that they could not bring themselves to see an alternative.
Bukharin's biographer Stephen F. Cohen, who had an influence on
Gorbachev, the rehabilitation of Bukharin, the much discussed
"Bukharin alternative," and the whole glasnost campaign, said himself
that he still could not see another course that would have prepared the
country for war with Hitler. This hard standard of measure was necessarily the context of discussion. As one post-Soviet Russian history textbook puts it, "The Great Patriotic war was a cruel exam for the Soviet
economy, an exam which was passed."

The Great Turn also struck like thunder in Comintern affairs.
Having gone left with Zinoviev and the "Bolshevization" at the Fifth
Comintern congress in 1924, then right when Bukharin was its
President, from 1925 to 1927, the Comintern now went left again,
reviving the Zinoviev slogans from 1924. The social democrats of the
world were once again described as "social fascists," the left wing of
the fascist movement, with whom no Communists could honestly cooperate. Molotov, Stalin's closest associate, promoted the line once
associated with Zinoviev. The Comintern was said to be entering its
"third period" of activity. The first had been the period of revolution,
1919–1923; the second of stabilization, 1924–1927; the third would
be a return to militant revolutionary action. Communists all over the
world were urged to engage in radical acts they would have called
"sectarian" a year before. Indochinese Communists staged an armed
insurrection in 1930. American Communists made strikes to organize
the unorganized, ignoring AFL strictures against "dual unionism."
German Communists supported a referendum to remove the Social
Democratic local government in Prussia. Joining with the Nazis who
initiated the poll, they renamed it a "red referendum."

From his exile on Prinkipo Island off the Turkish coast, Trotsky
criticized the madness of the Third Period line and made urgent
appeals for unity with the German Social Democrats. His idea was
that a united front of Communists and Social Democrats would revive
in Germany the tactics that had brought Communism in Russia to
power in 1917. Defending against the Nazi gangs was in his mind
comparable to defending against Kornilov; the Petrograd Soviet, he
said, had been a form of united front. He was not calling for an electoral bloc, which would have been useless at any rate, owing to the fact

that German governments had been ruling by decree since 1930. President Hindenburg would have been unlikely to permit a leftist united front to come to power. He hesitated before inviting the Nazis who, in the elections of spring 1932, had 38 percent of the vote. The ideas of Trotsky that many historians, including E. H. Carr, so admired were not what they seemed. They were not a means of stopping Nazism in the sense of saving the Weimar republic, but another attempt at a German October. The glasnost literature of 1987–1988 never weighed this point. It took the issue up and endorsed, generally, the criticism of the presumed suicidal policy of the German Communists, and therefore of Stalin. Stalin was in effect blamed for Hitler's rise to power. Perhaps another policy would have been better. But would it have kept Hitler at bay permanently?

Soviet foreign policy during the era of the Great Turn remained on a defensive track. It was designed to unhinge any potential coalition that might be arranged against the Soviet Union. There had been fear in 1927 that Piłsudski's Poland, with French and British encouragement, would essay another version of its 1920 invasion of the Ukraine. This, it was thought, might be accompanied by an invasion of the Soviet Far East by Chiang Kai-chek's Kuomintang. To ward this off, the Soviet policy was to appease Japan and cultivate her as a counter to China. In the west, the Soviets took advantage of the Kellogg-Briand pact of 1928, a pact to outlaw war, in order to advance a defensive bilateralism under their version of the pact, the Litvinov Protocol. In this way the Soviets got bilateral nonaggression pacts with Estonia, Latvia, Lithuania, Poland, Romania (without the Soviets recognizing the 1918 Romanian seizure of Bessarabia), Turkey, Persia, and Danzig. In 1932, the Soviets got nonaggression pacts with Poland, Finland, Estonia, and Latvia. The French had erected their alliances in east-central Europe partly to serve as what Clemenceau called a *cordon sanitaire*, a bulwark against Bolshevism (which the Soviets saw as a base for aggression against them). The nonaggression pacts unhinged the whole French policy. The Soviets added the crown in the edifice of their bilateralist policy in 1932 by a pact with France.

Success in the west was not matched in the east. Japan invaded Manchuria in 1931. The Soviets felt too weak to do anything about it. They offered to sell the Chinese Eastern rail line to Japan. The price dropped steadily as the negotiations proceeded over the next three years, from 650 million yen to 140. That gave the world a rather precise quantitative measure of the change in the eastern balance of power. Right up to Hitler's march into the Rhineland in 1936, Japan would remain the first concern for Soviet security.

The Far Eastern threat was balanced somewhat by the success of bilateralism in the west. But the Third Period line still maintained its momentum and tended to cut against the French. Of all the German parties, the Social Democrats were the most dedicated to improving relations with the French. Communists regarded them as traitors and preferred other groupings designed to put themselves on the right side of the national issue. In 1931 Heinz Neumann, Stalin's closest associate in the German party, managed to win the boss's support for the line of "national revolution" in Germany. This would have made possible Communist adhesion to a bloc of nationalist parties with a Revisionist, that is, anti-French, foreign policy. This move coincided with a high point of anti-French feeling in Europe. The Western powers were unhappy with what they saw as French intransigence on disarmament. They blamed the French obsession with security that kept them from accepting German equality of armaments. The British even vaguely blamed the French for the financial cirsis that took them off the gold standard. The Third Period Comintern policy, with its continued softness on German nationalism, was indirectly, perhaps unwittingly, contributing to this mood.

The advent of Hitler to power in 1933 was without doubt the greatest defeat for the Russian revolution as an international force. Trotsky said that it was the worst for the working class of the world since 1914, when the European Social Democrats had voted for war. It was the result, he said, of Stalin's neglect of the Comintern and his infatuation with Socialism in One Country. Stalin's people tried to brush this aside, but it was not long before they had to change their foreign policy around 180 degrees and begin to search for allies against Germany. Even so this did not happen before an inner-party crisis had forced another general change of direction on Stalin.

CHAPTER 10

The Great Purge and the Path to War

L aunching the planned economy on the basis of agricultural collectivization was in effect a decision to create a new society with a new working class and intelligentsia. It seemed to those who supported Stalin in 1927–1928 that there was no other choice. Only a modernized Russia could fend off the threat from Britain and France, possibly assisted by Poland and Japan, Romania, and others. It is ironic to note that Germany was not among the perceived enemies. The threat of a renewal of the allied intervention of 1919, as they saw it, could only be met by a return to the methods of War Communism. Stalin was attempting something grander than anything in Russian history, grander than the work of the Tsar Liberator, Aleksandr the Second, who freed the serfs; grander than Peter the Great, who made Russia a maritime trading nation; or even Ivan the Terrible, who made Muscovy into Russia. It was no accident that Stalin began to think of himself in terms of the great monarchs. He was the latest personification of what professor Miliukov had once called Russia's "critical state."

The civil war of 1918–1921 had originally made possible the Communist party's dictatorship over Soviet Russia. By 1928, Stalin had won the leadership of Lenin's party dictatorship by adroit navigation of the antagonisms between his rivals. The collectivization of agriculture was a second civil war that lifted Stalin to new heights of personal power over the party.

Even so, to feel fully secure in this regime, Stalin would, in the next few years, bring down Lenin's party dictatorship and put in its place a thoroughgoing police state, a regime of permanent civil war. Party Congresses, which had previously met yearly, met only in 1934,

93

1939, and 1952. Central Committee meetings became a rarity. Even the full Politburo met only on extraordinary occasions. Votes were taken by polling. The best measure that scholars have been able to adduce about the relative influence of the different leaders is the record of frequency and length of visits to Stalin's office. By this measure Molotov and Lazar Kaganovich, who logged the most time, enjoyed the most favor. The omnipotent police, whose investigations and arrests were followed daily in the press, reported directly to Stalin.

He was still putting finishing touches on the new system of rule when World War II broke out in 1939. In the years of the Great Purge Stalin would rerun his previous victories over Trotsky, the Leningraders (Zinoviev, Kamenev, and others), and the Right (Bukharin, Rykov, and Tomsky). Not that they had to be defeated so many times. After the turn of 1928, none of them counted for anything at the pinnacle of power. But they were capable of influencing the intellectual life of the party, by an article here or there that demonstrated their fitness to participate in the making of policy. Except for from the exiled Trotsky, they capitulated and renounced opposition, so it was difficult to exclude them entirely from the political life of the country.

Stalin's task was to keep his own group, not many of them mental giants by comparison with the leaders of the opposition, immune to the latter's influence. Even after victory over all the oppositions, Stalin had constantly to firm up the Stalinists, test their loyalty to him and their animosity toward his critics and detractors, real or imagined. The Stalinists were not churning out books and articles, nor were they charismatic speakers. Moreover, after their having emerged as the victorious faction, it was even doubtful that they would follow Stalin through all his turns or do enough to increase his power. He had to wonder about their deepest loyalties and about their real estimation of him as a Bolshevik, whether they really thought him intellectually superior to a Trotsky or a Bukharin, or even a Zinoviev or a Kamenev. He knew that they were aware of material in the émigré press, the Trotskyist *Bulletin of the Opposition* and the Menshevik *Socialist Courier*, which had more interesting things to say about the situation in the country than the Soviet press.

The most powerful voice was Trotsky's, writing from exile in various places, Prinkipo Island in the Sea of Marmora at the Dardenelles, then Norway, France, and finally after 1936, Mexico. He published a three-volume history of the revolution, pamphlets on many controversial issues of international Communism, almost daily articles on the Soviet scene, and a book against Stalin, *The Revolution Betrayed*, in 1936. At the beginning of the war, he was working on a biography of

Stalin. Trotsky was not always opposed to everything Stalin did. He called the turn to collectivization a "centrist zig-zag," in 1928, not disapprovingly. He claimed that the previous economic critique of the Zinoviev-Trotsky Joint Opposition "had fructified developments," but Stalin could not be trusted to stay with it. Then, in 1930, he said the zig-zag had become "an ultra-left course" and called for a "timely retreat." This was within a few days of Stalin's speech on "Dizziness with Success," in which the General Secretary called for a slowing of the tempo of collectivization. Trotsky bounced back and forth, but so did Stalin.

Trotsky had never capitulated as had all the other left oppositionists, Radek, Rakovsky, Zinoviev, and Kamenev. After his resistance to collectivization was overcome in 1929, Bukharin came out perversely against the "Right Danger." He praised Stalin and renounced his old ways. By 1934 Stalin would make him editor of *Izvestiia*. He told Stalin frankly that he knew that he could be crushed politically, but that it was not a good idea, in view of his unswerving loyalty, at least lately. But Stalin knew that, even as a Stalinist, Bukharin had come close to making common cause with a number of small critical groups. In 1928, while meeting with Kamenev, he called Stalin a "Genghiz Khan" and "a petty oriental despot" and said that the differences among the oppositionists, left or right, were as nothing compared to the differences of all of them with Stalin. That was the way Stalin saw it as well.

Since Stalin had established himself largely as the ally of Bukharin in 1925–1927, associates of both men tended to lean temperamentally to the right. Some of Bukharin's did not follow his flip against the Right Danger and had to be disciplined in 1929. Mikhail Riutin, an editor of the military paper *Red Star*, was expelled in 1930, as were faithful Stalinists Syrtsov and Lominadze. Trotsky wrote an article comparing the French and Russian revolutions, in which he said that the Jacobins had been overthrown by a combination of right and left opponents. So, he thought, it must be with Stalin. The boss hears nothing but praise from those who "swear oaths of loyalty to the beloved leader, and at the same time, have at the back of their minds: how to betray to their own best advantage." Trotsky articulated Stalin's worst fears. Stalin, who read him assiduously, was in effect subjected to Trotsky's intellectual terrorism. *Pravda* even began to warn that the struggle against anti-party elements is waged "on two fronts."

In fact, Stalin did not need Trotsky or anyone else to point these things out for him. He had far better information about any potential disloyalty. At the same time, he was surrounded by people who did routinely call him a genius. In the end he was intelligent enough to doubt that anyone of Lenin's generation of leaders could genuinely admire him that much. He may have been mediocre in the company of those who write books, but he was far from naïve. A bad impression was created by those who professed personal affection for him. Kamenev, after submitting to him docilely in 1927, spoke publicly in 1934 of the danger of a Russian *vozhd* (*Duce*, supreme leader). Then, when Stalin took offense, he wept and begged for forgiveness, proclaiming his love for Stalin. This was a bad idea. Toadying and praise, personal effusions, made Stalin all the more suspicious. Serebriakov was right to say that "Stalin is too crafty to be deceived by flattery."

A larger group of Stalin supporters were expelled in 1932, including some "national deviationists" who made special claims on behalf of the Ukraine and Armenia. Trotsky and his family were deprived of citizenship in February; when he learned this Trotsky said in an Open Letter to the Soviet government: "Stalin has brought you to an impasse. You cannot proceed without liquidating Stalinism . . . it is time to carry out Lenin's final and insistent advice: remove Stalin!" By the end of the year Trotsky was in indirect contact with the Riutin-Slepkov group in Russia who composed a Letter of Eighteen Bolsheviks in fall 1932, at the same time that Riutin circulated a book-sized document. In this "Riutin platform," Bukharin was said to be right in economic policy (that is, collectivization had been a bad idea) and Trotsky right in matters of party democracy. Riutin called for peace with the peasants and reconciliation with the oppositionists. Stalin was an "evil genius" and "gravedigger of the revolution." His personal dictatorship must be ended at all costs.

A copy of the platform was sent to Zinoviev and Kamenev. Bukharin, Rykov, and Tomsky also saw it. Stalin could quite sensibly imagine them to be anticipating his overthrow. Trotsky and his son Leon Sedov, who maintained contact with the Riutin-Slepkov Eighteen, even carried out an earnest discussion about whether to assassinate Stalin. Sedov was unhappy that Trotsky preferred to drop the slogan "Remove Stalin!" (from the Lenin Testament) for "Down with the Personal Regime!" (from the Letter of the Eighteen Bolsheviks). Sedov thought that, "as the Germans say, once you say A, you have to say B." Once you call for the downfall of the personal regime, you are calling for Stalin's "liquidation," which certainly made sense in view of the Trotsky's famous Clemenceau Statement of 1927. Trotsky drew back from this, reasoning that it would only feed the thought that, if Trotsky were to return, it would be with sword in hand.

The matter of the Riutin platform came to a head at the Central Committee meeting of September–October 1932, when Stalin apparently suggested the party should shoot Riutin. But he was turned back by a grouping of his own Politburo supporters who were fearful of crossing this threshold. Riutin got only a 10-year prison sentence. They had been shooting recalcitrant kulaks, leaders of the peasant revolt, "wreckers," and others on a small scale for several years. But they did not want to shoot party leaders for their opposition views, even if they did want them ruined politically. Stalin had to put up with the idea that the Stalinists were moderate about opposition to Stalin, moderate even about calls for Stalin's removal.

After the plenum, the two most prominent secretaries, Kirov for Leningrad and Kaganovich for Moscow, tried to put their own spin on the situation. Kirov praised the work of the meeting and the rebuff dealt to the Eighteen and to Zinoviev and Kamenev, who were to be expelled. He seemed to regard the struggle with the opposition as a matter for the historians: "There was a time when we fought the left and the right. Now all those questions are decided." He said that collectivization had won the battle between socialism and capitalism, a battle that had been waged in the country since 1921. The oppositions were all defeated and counted for nothing politically. There was no point in pursuing them any further.

But Kaganovich said just the opposite: The oppositionists, having been defeated politically, were now going underground and resorting to criminal activity to accomplish their nefarious goals. They would be even more of a danger, since, in general, the closer the party and society gets to socialism, the more intense the class struggle becomes. This reflected the War Communist spirit of the last years, in which the struggle for socialism meant taking on the peasantry. This was a fight among Stalinists, between an easier regime and a permanent purge. There was no hint of any opposition to Stalin, only a difference about ways and means of dealing with his enemies. If there was such a thing as a Kirov line, it was one of complacency and *moderantisme*. Since Stalin and Kaganovich had been thwarted in dealing with Riutin, Kirov's approach would be followed, at least for a time. At the Seventeenth Party Congress of 1934, Stalin looked around, said that everywhere the Leninist line had been victorious, and that there was "no one left to beat."

In fact, an easier regime did result. In the following year, the economy looked a little better. The crop failures of 1932 had been the worst in recent memory. Nevertheless, Stalin had ruthlessly exported grain to maintain his line of credit in the west, even while that meant famine. There were good harvests in 1933 and 1934. The furious ransacking of homes in rural areas for jewels and gold (the "gold inquisition") was ended. Bread rationing was dropped. This "liberal spell" or neo-NEP characterized the moderate regime of the second five-year plan, with its many concessions to tradition and to the consumer. Oppositionists who had repented could recover a post somewhere and the semblance of acceptance in party life. Zinoviev was made editor for a time of the theoretical journal *Bolshevik*. Bukharin got *Izvestiia* for a mouthpiece. All they had to do was to praise Stalin and denounce their former comrades, especially Trotsky, in the most forthright terms. In return they could pronounce on the issues of the day, especially in foreign policy.

The turn to the right coincided with a sea change in the international situation with the advent of Hitler to power in 1933. The French sent feelers for an alliance to the Soviets in December 1933. When Poland made a pact with Germany in 1934, these became serious. The French began to think they would have to replace Poland, hitherto the center-piece of their alliance system, by the Soviet Union. The Soviets tried their best to hold on to a connection with Germany, but by the summer of 1933 it was obvious that all goodwill had gone out of the Rapallo relationship. With a heavy heart, Russians read translations of the passages in *Mein Kampf* where Hitler speaks of settling millions of German peasants in Russia.

The Comintern did not immediately alter the Third Period line. The French Communists had to break with it at the time of the Stavisky riots of February 6, 1934, when fascist demonstrations raised the prospect that France would follow Germany into a fascist regime. The French Communists proposed a united front of the left and a for-eign policy friendly to the Soviet Union. The front managed to turn back the French fascists by a general strike six days later. In Moscow, Bukharin and Radek saw this as the beginning of a worldwide move-ment against fascism. Molotov, who had in 1928 energetically removed Bukharin and his international co-thinkers, Jay Lovestone, Bertram Wolfe, and Isaac Deutscher, in pursuit of the Third Period Line, now looked foolish. Unity with the Social Democrats and other opponents of fascism was on the order of the day.

The new French foreign minister Louis Barthou sought to take advantage of this sentiment to press for a campaign of pressure on Hitler for an "Eastern Locarno," that is, a guarantee of Germany's eastern borders as the western ones had been guaranteed at Locarno in 1925. He hoped to enlist Britain, fascist Italy, and the Soviet Union, but also Poland and the other eastern states, Revisionist Hungary and

Bulgaria excepted. At the same time a pro-French agitation arose in the Soviet press around the idea of a rally against the "bestial philosophy" of Hitler fascism. Bukharin was a leading spokesman of the anti-fascist, pro-French line. He saw the rise of the united front in France as part of a general upsurge of leftist feeling in Europe, one that should logically result in governments that were hostile to fascism and eager to make common cause with the Soviets.

Then suddenly, in December 1934, came the news that Kirov had been assassinated. Bukharin denounced this as the work of his old archenemies, Zinoviev and Kamenev, the "Charlotte Cordays of the Russian revolution." They had not pulled the trigger, he said, but their followers and co-thinkers were so suffused with their poisonous views that they had been influenced to do so. Most of all, said Bukharin, they wanted to wreck the progressive pro-French foreign policy because it was leading to an anti-Hitler coalition in Europe. This in outline was the case made against Zinoviev and Kamenev in the first Moscow trial 18 months later. Stalin had only to follow the lines laid out by Bukharin, as in 1925. It was a rerun of the rout of the Leningraders at the Fourteenth Congress.

Louis Barthou had also been assassinated at the end of 1934, along with Yugoslav King Alexander, by Croatian terrorists, with help, or at least encouragement, from Mussolini and Goering. In his place Pierre Laval continued in the same vein, or so it seemed. A Franco-Soviet pact was signed in May 1935 at virtually the same time as a "Stresa Front" of England, France, and Italy was set up to pressure Hitler. But in June, the British ruined the Stresa Front by signing a naval treaty with Germany, allowing Germany to build a fleet 35 percent of the size of the British. The French and the Italians were badly let down. The 35 percent permitted to Germany by Britain struck the Soviets as being more than the Germans already had and perhaps enough to support an aggressive policy in the Baltic against Russia. German action in Norway in 1940 would show that this was not a fantasy. It was shortly after the Anglo-German naval pact that the first Soviet feelers went out to Germany for an improvement of relations. Soviet trade officials Bessonov and Kandelaki were sent to conduct talks in July.

Were the Soviets preparing to come to terms with Hitler just as they formed an alliance with the French? Naturally, they would have cooperated with the most passionate sincerity in any attempt to hem in Nazi Germany by diplomatic means, as envisioned by Barthou. The Stresa Front made good sense from the standpoint of national interest. But this can hardly suggest that, if this diplomacy were to fail, the

Soviets would ever have been ready to play the role of a continental war ally to Britain and France, one who, in view of France's "Maginot line mentality," her unwillingness to invade Germany, would in the end have to do the bulk of the fighting while her allies looked on from afar.

There was, moreover, a cogent Soviet criticism of the Barthou policy. In the view of some, the Stresa front was a Machiavellian affair because it implied that to get Italy's support, Mussolini was to be given a free hand to invade Abyssinia. Molotov warned that Bukharin's pro-French line was not a real solution. It was, he said, simply trying to make an imperialist deal of the nineteenth-century type. Ultimately security could only be assured by a continental understanding between Russia and Germany. True, Germany did not at present want this understanding. But a repeat of the Triple Entente as in 1914 would only mean playing the imperialists' game. Molotov made the point more clearly when Germany invaded the Rhineland in March 1936. In an interview with the Parisian *Le Temps*, he said that while there were many in the Soviet government who felt it necessary to oppose Germany, there were also those who wanted to improve Soviet-German relations. This was a frank admission of a struggle over foreign policy in the Soviet leadership.

Which side did Stalin favor? Historians have no consensus. Some argue that he left foreign policy entirely to his Foreign Minister Maksim Litvinov, who sought to bolster the Franco-Soviet alliance and build collective security against the Nazi threat. The Comintern policy of the Popular Front, proclaimed in 1935, was a backup. In this view Stalin only agreed to a pact with Hitler in 1939 when the Anglo-French policy of appeasement gave him no alternative. Others take the view that Stalin was always eager to come to terms with Nazi Germany as Molotov suggested. Some say that this was because of a natural affinity for the German dictatorship and the Rapallo tradition in Soviet foreign policy. Scholars who have seen Politburo correspondence between Stalin and his associates have not been able to clinch the matter one way or the other. Was he weighing the alternatives? Or did it make sense for him to bend every effort to get the British, the French, and perhaps the Poles to balance Nazi Germany, if possible with a minimum of Soviet commitment, perhaps even to come to terms with Germany after the others were committed? If so, was this a Stalinist or merely a Russian policy? We will return to these things when we consider the Hitler-Stalin pact of 1939.

In August 1936 came the trial of Zinoviev, Kamenev, and the Leningraders, the "Trotskyite-Zinovievite Terrorist Center." The prosecution described a plot that had begun with Riutin in 1932 for the assassination of Soviet leaders such as Stalin and Kirov. Molotov was not on what came to be known to the foreign press as the "honors list" of the so-called victims of the so-called plot. The conspirators' objective, it was said, was the partition of the Soviet Union together with Germany and Japan in return for installing them in power. On the precedent of earlier trials, it seemed that this one was aimed against opponents of the current line in domestic and foreign policy.

It was a trial of which the Bukharinists could approve. And Bukharin did approve, except for the unfortunate fact that he and Tomsky were themselves mentioned in some of the testimony as being in touch with the conspiracy. Was the purge turning against Bukharin? When Tomsky read of the testimony in the papers, he drew the right conclusions and shot himself. No doubt imagining himself as a future defendant, he took a shortcut. The papers announced the opening of an investigation into Bukharin's possible connection with the plot. But there was Politburo resistance to turning the purge against Bukharin. In September a meeting of the leadership in Stalin's absence decided to drop the Bukharin investigation "for lack of evidence." A grouping of politburo liberals, Kossior, Eikhe, Chubar, Postyshev, and others, had saved Bukharin. This meeting also apparently took the decision to intervene in the Spanish civil war.

It was like 1932 with Riutin. This was shown in a letter that Khrushchëv released at the time of his secret speech on Stalin's crimes in 1956, a telegram from Stalin's vacation retreat on the Black Sea coast. It demanded that Nikolai Yezhov, for whom the events of the next year would be called the *Yezhovshchina*, be brought in to head the investigation of the various plots. "We are four years behind in this matter," said Stalin. Four years: that would be the Riutin affair in 1932. The "liberals" had saved Bukharin as they had once saved Riutin. Yezhov was brought in and the arrests were stepped up. Over the winter the shipments to Spain got more sparse, and Soviet efforts there wound down in the spring of 1937, even as the Communists and their allies carried out a purge of the Spanish left.

The great purge followed the outlines of the struggle against the left in the 1920s. It was a struggle first against the left, as with the Leningraders in 1925–1928, and then the Bukharinists in 1928–1929. Both times it was easier to defeat the left. Perhaps one can say that the natural drift in the leadership was toward moderate policies, the NEP and the neo-NEP. Some have said that this was also because the policies of the left were advanced by less-attractive personalities who frightened the party and struck it as alien. In this view, it cannot have helped the internationalist-minded left to be led by so many who were Jewish:

Trotsky, Radek, Zinoviev, Kamemev. In any case, pulling against the "nativist" right was much harder and each time required a more violent turn. But Stalin was capable of these.

Spain was more Bukharin's cause than Litvinov's. The aim of Litvinov was to enlist Britain for a collective security bloc against Hitler. He wanted to cultivate British conservatives such as Churchill and Duff Cooper who were urging a grand alliance with the Soviets. Litvinov did not want to frighten them with the specter of a red republic in Spain. One account has Maisky, the Soviet ambassador to London, telling Churchill of the whole lurid purge plot, and Churchill, perhaps sincerely, perhaps humoring Maisky, replying that the scales had fallen from his eyes. In his account of the trials in *The Gathering Storm*, Churchill says of them that they were terrible, "but, I fear, not unnecessary."

Spain caused a two-year pause during which a modest anti-appeasement campaign in Britain, led by the Churchill-Eden group, began to gain an audience. But Stalin continued the turn against Bukharin. In January 1937 a trial of The Anti-Soviet Trotskyite Bloc, a "reserve center" of the original conspiracy, tried Radek, Sokolnikov, and others for a plot to make war on Germany. This was in a different tone from the first trial. Molotov was back on the "honors list" of the victims. Most of the defendants were shot, but both Radek (who was the Bolshevik most closely associated with good Soviet-German relations and the Bismarck tradition in Germany) and Sokolnikov (who personified good trade relations with Britain) were not. They each got 10 years for their high treason.

After the shooting of Tukhachevsky and some other generals in June 1937, the Bukharin trial finally arrived in March 1938. Bukharin had been prepared in prison for over a year. He, Rykov, and others were featured as ringleaders of the "Anti-Soviet Bloc of Rights and Trotskyites." Witnesses confessed to ridiculous crimes, as in the other trials. The same presumed plots with foreign governments were cited. But along with the by-then-familiar accusations there were new charges. The salient accusation with a foreign policy meaning was of a plot with Trotsky to "hamper, hinder, and prevent the normalization of relations between the Soviet Union and Germany along normal diplomatic lines." Bukharin and Rykov were shot. Two prestigious diplomats, Rakovsky and Bessonov, were spared. Rakovsky got a 20-year sentence for plotting with the British, while Bessonov received 15 years for plotting with the Germans. Molotov had won a victory over the Bukharin group and its pro-French line. The way was clear, in the party at least, to look for accommodation with Nazism.

Trotsky followed the trials and wrote constantly on them, even staging his own counter-trial in Mexico to demonstrate the absurd nature of the criminal charges against the defendants. He was out of Stalin's range for the moment, but his time was soon to come. Trotsky, Bukharin, Zinoviev, Kamenev, and Marshals Tukhachevsky, Yakir, and the other prominent personalities were the public face of the great purge. Yet it was not just these leaders who fell. Stalin's police reached down to seize "Trotskyites, wreckers, and double dealers" at every level of society, emptied out offices, pulled workers from the factory bench, rounded up suspects from schools, libraries, and hospitals. The purge was a crime against the whole Soviet people.

How many were its victims? This is a question that seems to fascinate any who come to the topic for the first time, and there was no authoritative answer until recently with access to Soviet archives. This evidence may be an official lie, but it is the record that we have. For political executions, the kind of which we have been speaking, the figure that historians now trust the most is 800,000 for the period 1934 to 1953. That would include the postwar purges; the "Leningrad Affair" of 1949; purges associated with the ruin of Rajk, Slansky, and other East European Communists; and shooting of people such as the economist Voznesensky, wives of some of Stalin's cronies, and some of his relatives whose company bored him on holidays.

Other respected estimates count that many just for the years 1936–1938. But these are as nothing compared to the estimates that were bounced around in the scholarly literature before the Soviet archives added their word. One often heard 9 million, sometimes as much as 65 million. Even now one can get back into the millions by considering the category of "excess deaths," people worked to death in the mines or forests, victims of famine, or of collectivization struggles or the like. It is rather dizzying. Eight hundred thousand strikes me as a large number. But for some reason it fails to satisfy. Many times, in speaking to various groups about this period, the question is asked and I render the tally of the archives as I have gathered it from those who have seen the records. There always seems to be a sense of disappointment. Asking myself why this is so, I have concluded that we want to compare Stalin's crimes to Hitler's and thus test what we have often heard: that Stalin was worse than Hitler. If I do not enter into a discussion of this quantitative riddle, it is because I am not sure of the utility of the conclusion, whatever it might be.

What was Stalin doing in his great purge? Certainly removing from his sight not only all those who had ever spoken a word of criticism against him but also all those he suspected of wanting to but keeping their counsel out of prudence. He pretended to be the Lenin of Today, but he was also wise enough to know that almost no one who had ever worked with Lenin shared this opinion. Getting rid of them was the only way to avoid their mocking eyes as they heaped false praise on him. Now he would have around him only those who did think him brilliant and indispensable. This is probably what Bukharin meant when he said that Stalin lusted to "to make himself taller and more brilliant." He became taller by reducing the height of those around him. What was the international meaning of the purges and the Moscow trials? Stalin was certainly clearing the decks of any possible opposition to an understanding with Nazi Germany. But he also needed to promote agreement between Britain and France to oppose Hitler. Soon he was to have all that he wanted.

CHAPTER 11

The Fate of the Revolution

How should we regard the regime of High Stalinism as displayed in the great terror? Was it a natural and inevitable outgrowth of the Russian revolution? If this regime was inherent in the nature of the revolution, why was such a vast terror required to attain it? Why did it have to devour such a large number of victims, with the most prominent leaders of the revolution and the civil war at the top of the list? These were not questions that could be discussed in the Soviet Union. Merely expressing any thought on this plane would have subjected you to attack by one of the "heroes of denunciation," someone who might not understand your motives, or who might have it in for you because of some slight, or who might want your job or your wife or husband, or might need to settle some other score, or advance his own qualifications as a hunter of "wreckers" and "Trotskyites."

Nor, curiously, was the question of the terror in the revolution one that much exercised the minds of contemporary observers in the West. They concentrated on matters closer to home: the persistence of the depression and the strife between left and right, the rise of the fascist powers who attacked Abyssinia, marched into the Rhineland, intervened in the Spanish civil war. In this perspective, Stalin's Russia was a kind of beacon of hope, an alternative model to depression and unemployment, a planned economy that seemed to have solved the problem of growth, a nation that began to be seen as the only serious potential counter to fascist expansion. It almost passed without notice that it was also as grinding a tyranny as any in the world.

Leftists, socialists, pacifists, students of the history of the revolution, and other thinking people might be considered cranks for raising the Russian Question, especially at such an indelicate moment. But many wanted to determine whether the Soviet Union had not merely turned into another European dictatorship, no different in essence than the fascist ones. They needed to decide whether revolutionary Russia had outrun the continuity that connected it to the ideals of nineteenth-century socialism and humanitarianism. They wanted to know whether there was anything in the Russian revolution that still deserved sympathy. Could Stalin's Soviet Union still be called socialist? Putting the question this way presupposed that socialism was not a criminal enterprise, as many of its enemies, not only the fascist ones, might think. Or were these enemies right to suppose that socialism is as socialism does?

Answers to these questions were passed down to the Cold War generations mostly by outcast revolutionaries of one sort or another who had found themselves objects of the revolution's wrath. Most did not regret the revolution itself but claimed that it had been betrayed. Anarchists, Left Communists, Workers' Oppositionists, adherents of the Workers' Truth, the Workers' Group, Trotskyists, Zinovievists, Bukharinists, and many others, who had once fought for the revolution and then become its victims, offered their testimony and their advice.

They created a robust literature of disillusionment in their attempts to answer The Russian Question: What is the nature of the Soviet regime? Was it a dictatorship of the proletariat, as advertised? Did the Soviet state itself need to be subjected to a class analysis? If the proletariat was no longer the leading class, had its place been usurped by a new class of bureaucrats, some kind of neo-bourgeoisie?

Russian anarchists who were eager allies of the Bolsheviks in destruction of the old Russian state in 1917, and who were among the first of its victims as the new state took its place, were the first to make this charge. Most of them had stuck with the reds through the civil war. Their break came in stages, some in 1918 with the first acts establishing state supervision of the economy, as with the formation of *Vesenkha*, the Supreme Council of the National Economy. Along with the Left SRs, they objected to the Brest peace and the compulsory grain requisitions of spring 1918. Then they learned of Lenin's enthusiasm for state capitalism. Some left Russia in 1921 with the defeat of the Kronstadt rebellion and the suppression of Nestor Makhno's Ukrainian anarchist guerilla army. Many simply converted to Bolshevism.

Others writing from exile, G. P. Maksimov, Emma Goldmann, Aleksandr Berkman, and Volin (Vsevolod Eichenbaum), denounced the Soviet bureaucrats and their professed theory of state capitalism.

It was a natural fit for the anarchist theory of the state, according to which capitalism did not conquer by trade. The economic system, in the anarchist lens, is the result of the actions of the state, establishing and maintaining money, as one of the inspirers of the anarchist creed, Pierre-Joseph Proudhon, once called it, "constituted value." Marx was wrong, thought the anarchists, to think that cheap goods broke down all the "Chinese walls" obstructing the world market. In China, for example, it was not cheap goods, but gunboats. Similarly with the Bolshevik state, which cleared the way arms in hand for the regime of the NEPman, the kulak, and the petty bureaucrat.

The anarchist theories of the 1920s and 1930s were brushed aside by those who supported the Soviet state, unless they found themselves in trouble with the party, in which case they made good use of their insights. So it was with some of the losers in early faction fights, for example, Gabriel Miasnikov and A. A. Bogdanov, who led party factions critical of the NEP and supported strikes in 1923, with the result that they were expelled. Then they began to see the New Exploitation of the Proletariat as a question of a new exploiting class.

When Zinoviev and the Leningraders came out in opposition to the Stalin-Bukharin bloc in 1925, the idea of a Thermidorean degeneration and slippage in the direction of state capitalism began to appear in their documents. When they said that the ruling bloc was "Mensheviko-Ustrialovist," they were referring to the previsions of Nikolai Ustrialov, the White émigré who had said hopefully in 1921 that the Thermidorean Bolshevik regime would soon be undermined by the NEPman, the kulak and the bureaucrat. Years later, after Zinoviev's capitulation to Stalin, French Zinovievist Albert Treint, who had got the leadership of the French party in the "Bolshevization" at the Fifth Comintern Congress in 1924, only to lose it when Zinoviev fell, argued that the slogan of Socialism in One Country and the Comintern policy of National Bolshevism gained a complete victory over revolutionary internationalism in 1928 when the Zinoviev-Trotsky opposition was defeated. Treint's argument comes through strongly in Ruth Fischer's famous and influential book of 1948, *Stalin and German Communism*. Treint concluded that the state capitalist trend was firmly entrenched in Soviet Russia, Nazi Germany, and New Deal America. So there was such a thing as a distinctly Zinovievist theory of the degeneration of the Soviet Union.

Trotsky later became famous for the thesis of the Thermidorean degeneration of the Bolshevik party, which ruled in a Soviet Union that still had to be considered a workers' state. But this usage was originally that of Professor Ustrialov. Trotsky himself called the NEP

a Thermidor in 1921, one in his view carried out by the "Jacobins,"
that is, by Lenin and Trotsky. But he soon dropped the idea. Not much
more was heard about it until Zinoviev took it up in 1925 as a criticism of Stalin-Bukharin. At this point, before he had gone into
opposition, Trotsky rejected the notion of a Thermidorean trend and
broke with those who entertained it, even after his exile in 1929. He
only embraced (or rather, re-embraced) the Thermidor concept after
Hitler took power, an event he called the greatest defeat for the working class since 1914. The Communist Third International was discred-
ited as the Social Democratic Second International had been in the
world war. There was no alternative to building a Fourth International
of new Communist parties.

In Trotsky's *Revolution Betrayed* of 1936 the Soviet Union is
described as a regime run by a Thermidorean bureaucracy, thus a
"degenerate workers' state." He urged the overthrow of the Stalinist
bureaucracy. But, he was asked, can the workers get along without a
bureaucracy? His answer was that they might abolish the "bureaucracy" but still need an "administration," a distinction that is not intui-
tively grasped. Nevertheless, despite the Soviet Union's bureaucratic
degeneration, it was still a workers' state, he thought, and thus
deserved unconditional support against enemies.

Others came to different conclusions. French philosopher Simone
Weil called the USSR a state "neither capitalist nor proletarian." In
1938–1939, German Social Democrat Rudolf Hilferding, whose early
work on imperialism was read widely before World War I, suggested
another designation. For him, state capitalism could not pass the test.
One could hardly speak of capitalism in the absence of private property
and a market mechanism. Nor could one say that the Soviet Union was
really ruled by a bureaucracy. Stalin had shot too many bureaucrats.
Hilferding decided that Stalin's Russia should simply be called "totalitarian state economy." Taking this a few steps further one might con-
clude that a state that is neither capitalist nor proletarian represents
an illustration of the principle of the autonomy of the state.

During the years of the Hitler-Stalin pact, the idea of a totalitarian
affinity between Stalinism and Nazism gained a certain currency
among Menshevik exiles and other socialist opponents of Soviet
Communism. Around this time other anti-Stalinist Marxists embraced
the idea of Bureaucratic Collectivism, a term used by Ivan Craipeau,
James Burnham, and Max Shachtman. For this, one had to imagine
that the events of 1917 had seen a "bureaucratic revolution," something absolutely new in history, a result of a movement that was the
creature of a bureaucracy, a new class that was bound to grow and

prosper. Both Totalitarianism and Bureaucratic Collectivism would later take hold as the Cold War transformed the world scene.

The Hitler-Stalin pact inspired an Italian writer, Bruno Rizzi, to argue, in a work titled *Bureaucratisation du monde*, that Nazi Germany, Soviet Russia, fascist Italy, and New Deal America were all examples of a new world trend, a "managerial" state and economy. The "four great autarchies" were bound to vanquish the old-fashioned imperialist states France and Britain and divide the world into economic blocs. There was no more room for the capitalists or for the Jews who required free trade and a cosmopolitan world. Rizzi pinned all his sociological generalizations on the international relations of 1939–1940. The United States, in his view, should not support decadent Britain and France but instead lead a new Holy Alliance of managerial dictatorships. A good deal of Rizzi's thinking appears in the work of James Burnham, whose ideas were outlined in his 1941 book, *The Managerial Revolution*. Burnham, like Rizzi, thought the fascist powers to be the more modern. He predicted their rapid military conquest of the world and advised adjustment to the inevitable. George Orwell thought Burnham to be a worshipper of the accomplished fact, or even the seemingly accomplished fact. He predicted, correctly, that there would be new future Burnham inevitabilities as the world nullified the previous ones.

After the war was transformed by the entrance of the United States and the Soviet Union, not much was said about these theories, although some non-Communist leftists continued to do variations. After the war, the rise of Soviet-American antagonism prompted an audition for "red fascism" and some other less-promising efforts. But these did not take hold. In the 1950s, the Yugoslav dissident Milovan Djilas published *The New Class*, an attempt at a reinstatement of the bureaucratic theory of Communism. Of all the writers in this genre, Djilas made perhaps the least attempt to interpret events. He also held that the "new class" had developed, not out of the intelligentsia as a whole but only from the Bolshevik party. Similar notions underlay the ideas of Mikhail Voslensky about the *Nomenklatura*, a term for the roster of Soviet bureaucratic entitlement. This may have inspired glasnost writers such as Boris Kagarlitsky, who called the USSR a "partocracy."

Criticism of the Soviet system for many required a sociological spin. A student of history who takes ideas seriously might want to know how and when the bureaucracy arose and whether this discourse has anything to do with Western theories of bureaucracy essayed, for example, by people such as Max Weber. Bureaucracy might be the result of the failure of the revolution or the result of the revolution itself. But it is also fair to ask if bureaucracy can be traced to any inherent tendencies of Marxism or of the nineteenth-century intelligentsia.

Before the revolution, as we saw in Chapter 2, it occurred to some that the nineteenth-century Russian intelligentsia itself was the nascent form of a new state bureaucracy. The anarchist Bakunin warned that the German Marxists, if they ever came to power, would organize society "under the direct command of state engineers who will constitute a new privileged scientific-political class." The Russian Jacobin populist Pëtr Tkachëv thought that education was the real source of class differences. More basic than the antagonism of lord and peasant or bourgeois and proletarian was the antagonism of the educated and the uneducated. He advocated rigid democratic control of schools at every level. If necessary, hold the bright students back! A populist of the 1880s, Yuzov-Kablits, argued that the intelligentsia should be defined economically, that is, by intellectual work. Perhaps education itself was a kind of capital.

The brilliant Polish-Russian radical Jan Wacław Machajski asserted this in the course of his indictment of socialism as the ideology of the intellectual worker. This, he thought, was the key to the evolution of the European Social Democracy, which turned the workers away from direct action in strikes and toward parliamentarism. "Intelligentsia socialism," said Machajski, would never overthrow an existing state for the sake of the emancipation of the working class, but always seek compromise through what we would now call the institutions of the welfare state. Machajski turned out impressive works to demonstrate his ideas and was read widely at the turn of the century, especially by social democrats. His major work, *The Intellectual Worker* of 1906, contained a dense economic argument suggesting that Marx had constructed his reproduction formulas in *Capital* to put aside a part of the product for the intelligentsia, according to the law of the "perpetual incommensurability of social product and social income."

But Machajski was mainly criticizing the parliamentarism of European social democratic Marxism. In 1918 he made his peace with Bolshevism, which he saw as an antidote to the social democratic trend. Nevertheless, Machajski has been discussed widely as a presumed key to the sociology of the Soviet workers' state. Perhaps he is, or perhaps even more than that. His ambitious social democratic intelligentsia might have a branch in Poland or Russia, or in any other country. Every country needs professional and technical specialists, white-collar workers, managers, directors, superintendants, and engineers. They might be spoken for by Marxism, but in the nineteenth century they were most eloquently spoken for by Saint-Simon and Comte. When Bakunin criticized Marx, it was for reformulating the socialism of Saint-Simon, in his view the true ideologue, the patron saint of the "savants" as a class. Saint-Simon's socialism was a frankly stated scheme for promoting the leadership of scientific intellect in a society that is rationally planned and directed. *Dirigisme*, as this idea is usually called, only means planning. One can plan anything. One can plan greater profits. Moreover, instead of lamenting the rise of the intelligentsia with Bakunin, Machajski and all the other critics of bureaucracy, one can even celebrate it.

It is ironic that so many leftists rejected the idea that the Russian revolution had left to the world a socialist state, when the fact was always accepted without difficulty by the Western business press. Leftists did not want socialism to have to take responsibility for Stalin's crimes. They thought that shifting the terms would solve the problem. It is nevertheless worthwhile to ask whether those who denied the socialist nature of the Soviet Union were relying on a definition of socialism as an extreme and thoroughgoing democracy rather than simply a publicly owned economy. Marx may have started this when he denounced the "Prussian socialism" of Rodbertus, and later Lassalle's flirtation with Bismarck. His followers rejected the *dirigisme* of Saint-Simon and Comte and the "state socialism" of the Bismarckian welfare state. There is certainly, in my opinion, some intellectual filiation between these nineteenth-century ideas and twentieth-century thoughts about bureaucracy. But in the Marxist tradition, where socialism is inseparable from democracy, there is a temptation to define it as a regime of rigid democratic equality.

Marx himself cautioned against this. In the *Critique of the Gotha Program* (1875) he objected to the German Marxists promising a regime of equality, or even worse, one of "equality of classes." The transcendence of capitalism will not bring equality, he insisted. There will be wage differentials even under the dictatorship of the proletariat whose watchword will be "to each according to his work." Stalin knew the critique of the Gotha Program well and cited it often against those who complained about inequality. Even Trotsky could not say he was wrong, but only that he learned the lesson too well.

It is also worth asking whether egalitarian passions did not create an unnatural preoccupation with bureaucracy. Perhaps bureaucracy is nothing degenerate but only, as Machajski had to admit, the natural growth of the intellectual workers as a class. The intelligentsia is a leading force in modern society (not just Soviet society), not because of any usurpation but because of the advance of science and technology, which causes society to require its services. A rapidly modernizing society appears to be in the throes of an intelligentsia revolution. Stalin saw his draconian dictatorship as the guarantor of the proletarian character of Soviet modernization, but he also allowed that "every ruling class must have its own intelligentsia." Since the rise of Stalinism coincided with the rise of Soviet modernization, the thought has persisted that he was in some figurative sense the instrument of the new ruling class, the "Thermidorean bureaucracy." That would make it, rather than he alone, the author of his crimes. Is this consistent with the actions of the intelligentsia after he was gone? It was proud of the national achievements of the Soviet regime. But did it cry out for more terror?

One might say that the intelligentsia, educated society, is the natural leading stratum under socialism and that socialism so far has been more of a nationalist idea than an internationalist one. But one cannot restrict the vistas of the intelligentsia to those of Russian Communism. In 1988–1991 the Soviet intelligentsia clearly made a market choice. The ways of the intelligentsia are not easily understood. Can it be that historical Stalinism is resistant to class analysis and sociological explanation?

CHAPTER 12

The Hitler-Stalin Pact, 1939–1941

T he Soviet nonaggression pact with Nazi Germany came only days before the outbreak of World War II. It used to be said that this unleashed the war and, from the standpoint of the Cold War that followed, that the pact unleashed the Cold War as well. As with the broader question of the origin of World War II, the farther away from it we get, the less the historians agree about the 1939 pact. At the risk of oversimplifying their views, developed in many absorbing and educational studies, one might say that there are two general trends of argument.

The first stresses the Western appeasement of Hitler. The Soviets preferred to combine with the Western democracies to stop the Nazis, it is said, but found they could not. Britain and France failed to defend the Treaty of Versailles and permitted the Nazis to occupy the Rhineland. They resolved to let the Spanish republic go down before Franco. They watched passively as Austria was absorbed into the Reich and helped enforce the Nazi partition of Czechoslovakia at Munich. Even after British and French guarantees to defend Poland against German aggression, they negotiated with the Soviets in a way that did not inspire confidence. The Soviets walked the last mile to get an alliance but, in the end, reluctantly concluded that they had no alternative but to buy time in anticipation of the inevitable future conflict by coming to terms with Hitler.

The other trend is rather the opposite. It considers Soviet appeals for collective security against the Nazi threat and the Comintern campaign for the Popular Front against fascism to have been facets of an elaborate Stalinist ruse. The Soviets never had any intention to participate in Western efforts against Hitler. They were ideologically set against alliance with the former Entente imperialists. They preferred the Rapallo orientation since 1922 (or perhaps since 1920, when they started to help clandestine German rearmament). The West was naïve to think that the Soviets were available for action against Nazism. A pact with Hitler, on the other hand, promised territorial gains in the east that Stalin could never expect from the Western powers. Agreement with brother totalitarians was the only real aim of Stalin's policy. In the end he preferred to trust Hitler.

There would be no point in knocking down these two straw men. In fact, elements of both interpretations are plausible and fit the known facts. In addition, much can be learned from previously unknown materials that continue to appear. In the end, however, the facts do not speak for themselves. One must appreciate the differences of national interest and resist giving Soviet ideology an independent and artificial role. No need to ask whether Stalin thought in terms of ideology or *realpolitik*. Realism is possible for any devotee of an ideology. Roosevelt's realism did not make him any less a liberal.

True, British and French appeasement could not inspire Moscow's confidence. But it would not be right to say that the Soviets were never available for cooperation with the West. They were available when the French sought to erect an encircling bloc around Nazi Germany in 1934–1935. They wanted diplomatic pressure on Hitler to agree to a guarantee of Germany's eastern borders. Stalin and the rest of the leadership would have loved this "eastern Locarno," which would have provided the context for the Franco-Soviet alliance of 1935. It would not have been a coalition for war against Nazi Germany, but merely for diplomatic pressure. Behind French policy Bukharin and Radek thought they saw social forces linked to the popular upsurge of 1934 on the French left against fascism. They urged the Soviet Union and the world to prepare for a long struggle against the "bestial philosophy." Molotov argued repeatedly against this that even diplomatic combinations against Hitler would not work. Hitler could not be deterred. The Soviets must come to terms and avoid war.

When the French project collapsed in 1935 with the Anglo-German Naval Pact, Molotov's arguments began to sound more sensible than Bukharin's. Even so, the Soviets were still available for projects to deter Hitler. But not to fight him, especially not to fight him alone. At Munich the idea of a four-power pact to settle European affairs once more came center stage in the Wwest. For the Soviets this was poison; it implied agreement in the West to permit aggression in the East. Locarno, in 1925, had been such a four-power pact. It had made the Poles uneasy and the Soviets only slightly less so. But for the

Soviets there had been a silver lining in the "reinsurance treaty" of 1926 with Weimar Germany. This seemed to suggest that Germany and Russia could agree at the expense of Poland if revision in the east was ever in prospect.

The ephemeral four-power pact of 1933 again threatened Poland, but this time Hitler broke off cooperation with Russia, soothed Piłsudski, and made an agreement with him in 1934. For the next five years, the Poles were on board Hitler's train. For the Soviets this naturally raised the specter of a possible German-Polish campaign into the Ukraine at a time when the old links of Soviet Russia to Germany were being severed.

From the Soviet viewpoint, the Nazi propaganda about a world struggle against Communism was only too frank. On the one side, a world Popular Front spreading its tentacles out from Moscow into Spain and China. On the other, the white knight of world anti-Communism, Hitler, aided by Italy and Japan. It was a clash of two worlds. Which side would the British and French take? From the Soviet viewpoint, the western appeasement line appeared to be a choice for anti-Communism, as they had supposed the British to have made in the 1920s. But even if this proved to be too rash a judgment, the Soviets were still watching the world break into economic blocs, with the Nazis assumed by all to have ambitions for further revision in the east.

Was there no way for diplomacy to avoid the impending clash? Bukharin's line meant preparations for war. Molotov suggested that the USSR could stay out of war if the Nazis and the Poles were to fall out. After Munich, the only hope for this hinged on the German demands for Danzig. Soviets feared that the Poles, after having supported the Nazi absorption of Austria and joined with the Nazis in partitioning Czechoslovakia, would be only too receptive to Hitler's plans for a Ukrainian campaign. But what if Hitler demanded Danzig as the price? Then the Poles might make a stand and the Soviets would have an opportunity for a pact with Germany at their expense.

The noisy Ukrainian nationalist campaign in the Czech-Slovak province of Sub-Carpathian Ruthenia was an indicator. Would Hitler lead these Ukrainian nationalists against the Soviet Union? Stalin complained about it in a speech on March 10, 1939. Less than a week later Hitler invaded Prague and ended the threat of the campaign into the Ukraine by tossing Sub-Carpathian Ruthenia to Hungary. That meant he would concentrate on Poland and, for that, he would need the Soviet Union. When the German and Soviet diplomats were signing the pact, Molotov raised a banquet toast to Stalin, saying that it was his speech of March 10, "so well understood in Germany," that had paved the way for the pact. The subsequent British and German guarantees to Poland offered the Soviets a rescue. If the Germans attacked Poland, the British and French might fight and Russia might stand clear.

Stalin's policy could only "work," that is, perform according to expectations, if both things happened: the Soviets got their pact with Germany and the French fought Germany in the west. The Soviets could not even count on their army being superior to the Poles in the east. If Germany and Russia were successfully to attack an isolated Poland, the Soviets and Nazis would be face to face in an occupation that would provide incidents to justify the long-anticipated German attack on Russia. But if the British and French were to declare war, there would be two German campaigns, in the east and the west. There would be two opportunities for the troops to bog down in trench warfare as in 1914–1918. As was to become clear, the Soviets did not reckon with the tank and its changes in warfare. They still expected what the French called *une guerre de longue durée*, hopefully one from which they could stand free. It was necessary for Soviet foreign policy to promote both a Western stand against Germany and a Soviet deal with her. The question of impending war was a matter of life and death. Mere greed for territory cannot explain the Soviet dilemma.

The Soviets thought the British and French guarantees to Poland were the solution. Their negotiations for alliance with Britain and France centered on the military preparations of their prospective partners. Could these have been expected to recruit Russia? Many on both sides realized that it was futile. For the Soviets, a pact with the British meant war; a pact with Germany meant watching the others fight. One is tempted to say that Stalin treated Britain and France the same way he treated Zinoviev and Bukharin in the 1920s. But any Russian diplomat, not only the despot Stalin, would have had to consider the same options. The former tsarist minister Durnovo had warned in 1914 that fighting the Germans would bring disaster (see Chapter 4). With Britain and France, Russia was in the wrong alliance. Molotov's line meant that Russia would not repeat 1914. Molotov was Durnovo's heir.

In coming to terms with Germany, Stalin and Molotov had planned to avoid the long war. But at first in the west, they got no war at all. The British and the French seemed to have seen through their plans. They declared war against Germany, but they did not fight. They even seemed to be waging an undeclared war against Russia. No wonder. The Soviets supplies and purchases in the east made Germany practically immune to the British blockade. Stalin contented himself with mutual assistance pacts with the Baltic States. But he thought he could attack Finland to get a border rectification that would make it impossible to attack Leningrad from across Lake Ladoga. When he did this, Britain and France seemed close to declaring war on Russia.

Stalin and Molotov had underestimated the rancor caused in the West by the Hitler-Stalin pact. On the right, admirers of fascism accused Hitler of betraying Western civilization; on the left, admirers of Communism broke with Soviet Russia. More and more, they all tended to see Russia and Germany through the same lens. For the British the military strategy of the war was going to be an indirect one: blockade, bombing, and subversion. It might also be aimed at Soviet Russia. In fact, Britain and France organized an expeditionary force to go to Finland to fight Russia. The French prepared troops in Syria to march to the Caucasus as Germany had in 1918. Turkey expressed sympathy. The British and French thought about attacking Baku after invading Iran and Iraq, moving up the Black Sea to rouse the Moslems in the Soviet Union. It would have been like the Allied Intervention of 1919 all over again. But it was all immense foolishness. Had Britain and France done these things, they would have been at war with both Germany and Russia.

When the Germans attacked Denmark, Norway, the Low Countries, and France in spring 1940, a sigh of relief went up in Moscow. They were glad to know that the Germans were not moving in their direction. But the German victory in France destroyed all their calculations for a long war in the West, the central premise of the Stalin–Molotov foreign policy. Despite its Machiavellian cleverness and its nuanced execution, it had failed miserably. The Nazi war machine would not bog down, not in Poland, not in France. Now it would be coming to Russia. Comintern propaganda, which had been calling the war imperialist and denouncing all the participants, began to change its tune. It eased its attacks on the United States. Reports of Barbarossa, the German plan for attacking the Soviet Union, began to filter in. Stalin knew about it almost from the moment it was drawn up.

Trotsky, in Mexico, sensed the change in the Soviet line and a lessening in the Soviet press of attacks on the Anglo-French "warmongers." He continued to be the fiercest Soviet patriot, as he had since the earliest days of his exile, even while he called for the overthrow of Stalin. He supported Stalin's efforts to retain the Chinese-Eastern railway in 1929. When Manchuria was invaded in 1931, he did not criticize the inaction of Moscow. He did not oppose the Soviet attempts to continue the Rapallo relationship with Germany even after Hitler had come to power. He granted that if he were to return to power, he too would seek to keep relations with Nazi Germany.

He did lament the breakdown of the world economy into economic blocs, warning that "planned autarchy is simply a new stage in economic disintegration." Against this no force would suffice save that of the United States, the most advanced capitalist economy. It could not sit still and watch the world fall apart. "Starving Japan," he wrote, "with six miserable divisions, grabs a whole country." The United States must open ways for itself peaceably or by force. The Japanese conflict with China created a community of interest between Soviet Russia and the United States. The American entry into the war would no doubt come by way of the Far East.

Stalin was Trotsky's most avid reader. As with Bukharin and Radek, while he wanted to reduce Trotsky's political influence to the zero point, he wanted his input on political matters. Curiously the policy line of Trotsky and Stalin was similar. Either Stalin imitated Trotsky or they were two minds that thought as one. But Stalin came to the point where he felt he no longer needed any of the old leaders for advice. When France fell, it became obvious that Hitler's attentions would turn to Russia. In the event of an invasion, Trotsky according to his traditional Bolshevism could be expected to issue a call for defeatism, as he and Lenin had during World War I. It was time to move the murder of Trotsky forward; it had been in the planning stage for some time. On August 21, 1940, an assassin in Mexico finally succeeded in carrying out the act. On his release from prison over 20 years later, he would be brought by Brezhnev to the Kremlin and quietly awarded the Lenin prize.

Stalin's murder of Trotsky was in a sense the last act of the Great Purges. All the other defendants in the Moscow trials had confessed to being part of a vast and tangled conspiracy, a kind of symbolic amalgam of all Stalin's presumed enemies, and all of it, according to the juridical fantasy, was led by Trotsky. In the Soviet mind of the Stalin era and for the most part to the end of Soviet regime, he was reckoned among the greatest villains in modern history. Even in the days of the glasnost campaign of Gorbachev, when all the victims of the Moscow Trials were rehabilitated, there was a curious confusion and indirection in the discussion of Trotsky. No one wanted to say that if Stalin had been wrong about Trotsky, Trotsky might have been right about Stalin.

How should we judge Trotsky's role in the Russian revolution from the perspective of the twenty-first century? He was certainly not an archfiend who killed Kirov, plotted assassination attempts on all the main Soviet leaders, organized wrecking in industry and agriculture, and plotted with Germany and Japan for the partition of the Soviet

Union, as was seriously maintained by Communists all over the world. He was, with many anarchists, Left Socialist Revolutionaries, and others, one of the most authentic voices of the revolution. He was the leader of the Petrograd Soviet, the director of the October insurrection, and the organizer of the Red Army. In the process of consolidating power and winning the civil war, he was the persecutor of anarchists and other radicals who had a different, but no less authentic, view of the revolution.

He sought to apply the model of the revolution abroad to achieve its victory as a world revolution. He tried, without success, to apply this model in Germany in 1923. He would have advised it once more for Germany in 1931–1932. He thought that France was in a revolutionary situation in 1936. The Spanish civil war was, he thought, a war by the Franco forces against the Spanish revolution. That is, he always regarded the foreign problems of the Russian revolution to be finally soluble only on the level of the world revolution. How could he have universalized the Soviet experience to this extent? The Russian revolution of 1917 had been a military mutiny in a lost war carried out by conscripted troops. This fact had given the revolution the support of the workers and peasants. This had made the Petrograd Soviet the key to the garrison and the power.

In applying the model of 1917 to other countries, Trotsky was, in effect, wagering that Bolshevik tactics would be relevant in entirely different situations. Could he have lived with the fact that they were not and gone on to lead the Soviet state in world politics, in foreign policy and war? On the evidence of his own acts as a Soviet statesman, there is little reason to doubt it. His destruction by Stalin was not because of any presumed fatal divergence from the course actually followed in domestic policy, with the exception of course, of the mass murder of Lenin's generation. Still less was it a matter of the irreconcilability of the theories of the Permanent Revolution with Socialism in One Country. It was a question of the individuals involved.

After the fall of France, the Soviets had scurried to take their allotted sphere of influence in the Baltic States and Bessarabia. In the process, they took Bukovina as well, "rounding out the Ukraine," Molotov called it. Hitler rushed to get in on the partition of Romania, giving Transylvania to Hungary in August 1940. Hitler said, "I am no longer going to let the Russians push me up against the wall." Stalin still thought there was room for more bargaining. But a meeting between Hitler and Molotov in November 1940 produced nothing. A few weeks later the finishing touches were put on Operation Barbarossa, the conquest of Russia.

The wisest people in the West, including Churchill and Roosevelt, never entirely gave up on Russia. They banked on Russian national interest not being able to live with German control of both the Baltic and Black Seas. Churchill told Stalin everything he could find out about plans for a German attack. A tide of warning engulfed Moscow, but Stalin rejected the appeals he got from Western governments as provocations. What other choice did he have? If they were right, it was all over at any rate; he and his coterie would be fighting for their lives while others watched from afar. What good would it do to make military preparations? He could only bank one last hope on the chance that Hitler was only applying pressure and would turn back after exacting some payment. And Stalin was willing to pay. He had before him the example of Lenin and Brest-Litovsk in 1918 as an idea of how much the country might give up and still survive.

In fact, Hitler was weighing alternate plans at that moment for a campaign into the Mediterranean and the Mideast. The whole war might have been kept on the level of a nineteenth-century expansionist struggle over "the Orient," rather than a titanic final battle against Marxism. But Hitler decided that the Mediterranean would have been another diversion, as the German air attack on Britain had turned out to be. He saw no reason further to postpone the final reckoning with Russia. In the spring and summer of 1941 the German army would roll over the Balkans and extend as far as Crete. This is just about the same distance from Berlin to Moscow and the terrain is easier. Everything else had been a preparation for the great moment, the culmination of the holy war against Jewish Bolshevism.

CHAPTER 13

World War II: Russia versus Germany

I t is said in some, but not all, memoir accounts that Stalin went into a terrible depression on learning of the German invasion of the Soviet Union. It must have been shocking to confront the bankruptcy of the foreign policy line that had led to the Hitler-Stalin pact. Despite all the machinations of Stalin and Molotov, they were not able to keep Russia out of the war. They had considered themselves the only ones who could accomplish that and the purges the price for their indispensable leadership. But now the Soviets were going to have the main fight on their own soil. They found themselves in the position into which they had been trying to put others. One might well have thought them Machiavellis without *virtù*.

One might just as easily have considered the German invasion a failure of Russian realist policy, a policy based on the idea of the balance of power with Russia the balance wheel. The problem was that Britain, France, and Poland could not balance Germany. Stalin's miscalculation on this was not any worse than that of the British and French leaders. Perhaps Stalin's (and Russia's) failure was inevitable, just as inevitable as their attempt to avoid their fate.

All the same, it was not such a bad fate. Russia could fight Germany. The Italian ex-Communist Angelo Tasca once remarked on the theory of Socialism in One Country that Russia was not a country but a continent. And the role of warlord was a natural for Stalin. He had been behaving for more than a decade as if the country were at war, and now it was. This meant that he was no longer the demiurge of a seemingly senseless oppression and terror, but a great national leader in the great anti-Axis cause of the whole world. The same methods that he had perfected in peacetime would now be put into the fight against

Hitler, an effort that the American General MacArthur was to call "the greatest military achievement in history."

It began with the Soviet forces overrun at every point where they were attacked. Hitler's armies went in three directions: in the north toward Leningrad; in the center toward Moscow; in the south toward the oil of the Caucasus and the coal of the Donbas. In about three weeks, the German forces reached Smolensk. But at this point they turned and bolted southward to take Kiev. Guderian and other German generals wanted to press on against Moscow, on the idea that the speed of the advance makes its own flank security. This classical military idea may have made sense within the spatial confines of Central Europe, but Russia was different. The Germans soon found that the great distances and the bad roads made it impossible for their impedimenta to keep up with their tank spearheads. This is not usually fatal except in the case of tanks and their need for gasoline.

Hitler decided on a more conservative course. He was convinced that Russia could not be defeated by racing to Moscow as Napoleon did. You had to destroy her armed forces by a complex series of encircling moves. The military blow at the start would shatter political cohesion. As German forces advanced, the unity of the Soviet state would collapse and Stalin would no doubt be overthrown by his own people. Hitler wanted to have significant forces in the south, in the best tank country, not only to get to the Soviet oil fields in the Caucasus but also to keep the Soviet bombers out of range of his own prized source of oil in Romania. As surprised as Stalin was that Hitler should attack him, no less was Hitler surprised that the Soviets proved able to fight. Guderian and some later German historians complained that, in failing to race to Moscow, the Germans had already lost. Moscow, an important industrial area and the nerve center of the whole rail network, was in their eyes the key to victory.

German troops spread into the Baltic States and Bessarabia and into the Ukraine, where in some cases they were welcomed as liberators. Stalin's initial orders were to hold every position everywhere. This was in keeping with the military élan he had tried to promote in the armed forces. But it meant that extended parts of the front were not only quickly lost but their defenders bagged by the vast sweeps of the German forces. This can also be partly attributed to the combination of a foreign policy of war avoidance and its territorial gains on the Baltic and in eastern Poland.

Later critics could argue that the foreword positions would have made better sense if the Soviets had used them to attack Germany in 1939. Large tank forces are more effective in the attack than in defense. But it was really only in 1940, with the fall of France, or perhaps 1941, with the great initial losses, that the Soviet army underwent a vast reorganization, the first of several, to put more tanks into armored units instead of parceling them out among infantry. Stalin's expecting to be able to hold everywhere may be put alongside general expectations for the defense, assuming that the Poles and the French would be able to defend. He did not reckon on the basis of the blitzkrieg model, but of the fighting of 1914–1918.

In July, Stalin appealed by radio to the Soviet people. He admitted the gravity of the situation and called for an unstinting effort to resist the cruel enemy. He raised the question of the 1939 pact. Could it be called an error? His answer was no. The country had bought time to prepare its military for the present test. The Germans would find that they would have no better time of it than Napoleon or the Kaiser. When Harry Hopkins visited Stalin later in the month, he found Stalin in good spirits and full of fight. He was told, "Give us some anti-aircraft artillery, some aviation fuel, and some other things and we can fight for three or four years." Hopkins was delighted. The United States was not at war but was already committing itself to help Russia.

Over the next four years, Lend-Lease aid to Russia was to be a much valued support to the Soviet effort. Supplies began to arrive almost immediately. Stalin had to politely accept some of the American tanks, inferior to the Soviet ones, but he was delighted to get bombers and fighter aircraft, of which he was sent some 20,000. The Soviets came to depend on U.S. jeeps and trucks, the latter crucial for the armored forces. Perhaps two thirds of all the trucks were from lend-lease, as was a good deal of rolled steel for tank production and telephone and telegraph cable, not to mention C-rations, especially those with Spam, which was greeted as a delicacy. Lend-Lease freed up as many as eight million Russians for other war work. Most of the supplies were brought in via Murmansk, Iran, and Vladivostok, with some flown to Siberia from Alaska. The high point was in 1944–1945. Aid from outside was certainly not the key to the Soviet victory but a much welcomed support from a powerful ally that helped to buck up Soviet morale.

Stalin also told Hopkins that the war of Nazi Germany against Russia was "not the work of the German bourgeoisie, the militarists, or even of the Reich as a body politic, but only the swift murderous passion of one man." Stalin had previously been thinking of Hitler as the instrument of the men in monocles and top hats that one saw in the sketches of George Grosz. He had thought it possible to deal with him by means of a combination of class analysis and what the bourgeois in the West called *realpolitik*. It was a sophisticated system of calculation. At some level, however, he was now coming to realize that history is also made, not by abstract nouns, but by real individuals with their own sometimes irrational ideas.

The German campaign resumed on the Smolensk road in September, and by October 15 the Germans were in the suburbs of Moscow. Standing on their tanks and peering through their field glasses, German officers could see the spires of the Kremlin. The Soviet government offices had already been evacuated eastward to Kuibyshev. Stalin had ordered the movement of some 1,500 factories from the various industrial centers to the Volga, the Urals, Kazakhstan, and other regions in central Asia, along with their millions of workers and managers, perhaps 10 million people in all. They did not always have proper facilities at the end of their journey. Sometimes machinery went into plants that had already been built pre-war. In the worst case, the plants had to be built around the machinery. Sometimes the workers did not have proper quarters and had to sleep at the plant while their housing was being built. It was a frenzy of feverish economic activity, but not really under the whip. Building socialism now had a deeper rationale than in peacetime.

Stalin called for all-out efforts from the Moscow population. Women drove trucks dragging tram rails torn up from the streets out to the edges of the city to be used as tank traps. Stalin insisted on holding a parade in Red Square to mark the 24th anniversary of the revolution. In his long speech he called on the Russians to remember the manly images of their ancestors, Aleksandr Nevsky, Dimitri Donskoy, Kuzma Minin, Aleksandr Suvorov, Mikhail Kutuzov, and Lenin. That was a sharp statement of the relationship between nationalism and Bolshevism, one that admitted of no contradiction between the two principles. There was a distinct Great Russian tone. At that point the Ukraine and the Baltic states were lost. It was now up to Russia herself. The troops raised a shout that echoed through the square as they marched directly to the front.

The rains came in October. Guderian said the weather and fierce Soviet defenses held him up at Tula, an arms production center south of Moscow. He was actually hoping for frost to get the tanks and trucks moving again. On December 6, he got his frost. The temperature quickly dropped to 40 degrees below zero. A few days later Hitler, realizing his troops were immobilized, had to order a suspension of fighting for the winter. Russia was saved for the moment. And, on December 7, the Japanese attacked Pearl Harbor. The Soviets were joined by a powerful new American ally.

The battle of Moscow had stopped the Germans. They surrounded Leningrad and subjected it to a siege that was to last almost three years. A million people died of starvation and disease. The Soviet forces nevertheless carried on through the winter in a vast counter-offensive at several points on the front, mobilizing partisan detachments to harass the German units. When an area was lost to the Germans, it was often put to the torch. Whole villages and little towns were destroyed. German power never extended more than a few miles from the main road, often a dirt track. The retreating Soviet forces urged the hapless population of a captured town to take to the woods. Many men and young women were able to do so, since they got weapons, supplies, and cadres from the rear to help organize guerilla war. The partisans raided the villages and towns they had evacuated and tried to kill the leaders who collaborated with the Nazis. They gave a lesson to all that, if the Soviet power was not victorious at the moment, it still existed.

The initial euphoria among many peasants about the German liberators began to wear off as they began to see that the Germans carried out mass shootings and deportations and meant to use them for slave labor. The peasants had not thought anything could be worse than the Communists who brought collectivization of agriculture, but now they were undeceived. In the captured areas, the Communist leadership was immediately shot. The Nazis took off any Jews for the camps in Poland and Germany. Acts against the occupying authorities, of which Communists made sure there were plenty, were severely punished. Usually 100 were shot for the death of any occupier. Reprisals against families were common. Several million ordinary workers were shipped off to work in Germany as virtual slave labor. The Nazis made no attempt to restore churches or to permit religious belief. At first there was a thought that the collective farms might be dissolved, imitating the Stolypin reforms and setting up a new class of pro-Nazi kulaks as a support for the occupation. But there was immediate resistance to this in the German General Staff, whose argument was that the collective farms were more efficient.

In the Baltic areas, in White Ruthenia (Belarus), in the Ukraine, the Germans refrained from any real appeals to the population offering national independence. Ukrainian nationalists nevertheless raised some military units in the chaotic conditions of the German-occupied areas where they had an opportunity to oppose both the Nazis and the Soviets. They were unhappy with the Nazis for having tossed Sub-Carpathian Ruthenia to Hungary in 1939, rather than using it as a base for their movement. They were unhappy with the Romanians, allies of the Nazis whose troops were part of the German front, for their absorption, with Nazi approval, of Pridnestria (the area along the Dniester River that enjoys independence under Russian protection today). But the Nazis never encouraged Ukrainian nationalism.

There was even a manifestation of anti-Soviet Russian nationalism among some who tried to revive the Cossack military heritage. There were some defectors from the Red Army itself, the most notable that of General Andrei Andreevich Vlasov, who took Nazi help in raising an army to overthrow the Communists. He had been a defender of Soviet Power since the civil war, a long-time Communist, a military advisor to the Kuomintang until 1939, and heroic and decorated defender of Moscow in 1941. Commanding the Second Shock Army in front of Leningrad in spring 1942, Vlasov and a great part of his unit were captured by the German forces. In captivity, he decided to switch sides, perhaps considering that he might be shot for surrendering with substantial forces, as General D. G. Pavlov had been in 1941 in similar circumstances. At any rate, Vlasov declared the formation of a Russian Liberation Army, but Hitler never let him do much beyond issuing some leaflets and posters. Only when things were quite hopeless, in May 1945, was he allowed to lead any troops against the Soviets. He was captured and executed in 1946. Vlasov was rather like a White general promising a democratic regime on the overthrow of Bolshevism. Like the White generals, he called for Russia One and Indivisible, and even referred on one occasion to the Germans as "guests," although he later wavered somewhat and allowed that he might let them have Crimea and some other areas. Hitler, not surprisingly, never trusted him and refused him any real support.

Some historians express surprise at the extraordinary political and psychological blunders of the Nazis in failing to make use of these factors that, they suppose, might have given the occupiers advantages. But this seems not to appreciate why the Nazis were there in the first place. Hitler was not trying to liberate the Russians from collective agriculture, or the nationalities from Russian rule, or even the Russians from Bolshevism. He was trying to colonize and annex European Russia. Liberation from the Soviet yoke might complicate the business of exploiting the new areas of the empire. As for the occupants, he meant to work them to death, move them into reservations, and settle their lands with German peasants.

Hitler was sure there would be no second front in the west. "Washington only consoles and assures," he said, "there is no actual second front. The proposal is to reckon on 1943." So Hitler threw everything into a march toward the Caucasus, reaching a "town that bears

Stalin's name" in July 1942. This was Stalingrad, set in a bend of the Volga. Soviet forces, with the river at their back cutting off the route for withdrawal, resolved to defend the city. An enormous battle of several months was mostly fought within the city limits. While it raged, the Soviets were able to bring up fresh units. They surrounded a force of about 330,000 Germans and pounded it down to about 100,000 when Field Marshal Von Paulus and 24 generals surrendered in February 1943.

Moscow had stopped the German advance; Stalingrad began the rout. This would continue until the defeat of the Germans in a massive tank battle at Kursk in July 1943, into which the Nazis threw about half the tanks in the German army. It ended with a crushing German defeat. It was all downhill from there. Soviets forces rolled on in fits and starts, but inexorably. After the allies landed in Normandy in June 1944, at about the time that the Soviets were liberating Minsk, diplomacy became much more important. Stalin meant to stay on good terms with Roosevelt and de Gaulle who had, in his view, championed the Second Front. He meant to observe the Western idea of the balance of power, to take whatever compensations he might be allowed, in view of the fact that the United States and Britain would be advancing their occupation armies in a way consistent with their own interests. He thought the victory of his armed forces would entitle him to take something in Iran, for example, comparable to the British oil interests there. He thought that the United States would see European affairs more his way than the British. He hoped to use his influence to please the United States in the Far East, even beyond defeating the Japanese Manchurian army with Soviet forces in summer 1945.

None of this was to take shape as expected. Instead there followed the Cold War. If this were a study of the origins of the Cold War, we would have to double back through our narrative and take more note of many events and issues that were not key to the outcome of the war: the Soviet massacre of thousands of Polish officers in Katyn forest in 1943, the Soviet deportation of Baltic and Caucasian nationalities, Soviet behavior with regard to the Warsaw rising of 1944, various discussions with the allies about the boundaries of 1941 and the activity of the Chinese Communists. These and other matters pertinent to the Cold War would take us beyond our story of the Russian revolution in the period before the Cold War. Let us leave to this period its own conceptual integrity lest we reduce the Russian revolution to a mere prelude to the Cold War.

Sometime between the battles of Stalingrad and Kursk, Soviet Communists began to get the idea that they might win this great struggle with fascism. For the first time they could tell themselves that the revolution had secured itself against its enemies. Was it a victory for the Communist party and for Stalin? In the Khrushchev era, when a critique of Stalin's mistakes had to be worked into all historical accounts, the Soviets liked to say that victory over Hitler was a victory of the party rather than Stalin: not an easy distinction and one that would have been thought curious to Soviet citizens at the time. Was the victory won by the five-year plans, as Stalin boasted in 1946? The German invaders apparently thought so. General Manteuffel, an armor officer, gave his own impression:

> The advance of a Russian army is something that westerners can't imagine. Behind the tank spearheads rolls on a vast horde, largely mounted on horses. The soldier carries a sack on his back, with dry crusts of bread and raw vegetables collected on the march from fields and villages. The horses eat the straw from the house roofs—they get little else. The Russians are accustomed to carry on for as long as three weeks in this primitive way, when advancing. You can't stop them, like an ordinary army, by cutting their communications, for you rarely find any supply columns to strike.

In this cinematic image we see the Germans confronting backward eternal Russia, the Russia to which Lenin referred when he continually reminded the comrades that they could not do what they pleased but had to remember always "we are dragging our peasant cart behind us" or "we are riding our old peasant nag." Except that this Russia had a modern industrial shield. There is a story that when the Germans and Russians were exchanging military data during the period of their pact, they each saw the other's tank works. The Russians kept asking to see the "latest" tank. This panicked their Nazi hosts, who thought, "they must have something better." They did. It was the T-34, by consensus of the German generals the best tank in the war. In the Cold War it saw service in Korea and much later in Angola in 1975.

Even these days, if you travel around the Russian countryside, you will still often find a T-34 monument in a prominent place in the public square of a little town. It had good armament, thick armor, a reasonably low silhouette, and speed equal to any of the German tanks. It had better maneuverability and better ease of maintenance for being a simple machine. And it was turned out of the factories like hotcakes. It was a homely symbol, perhaps the best symbol, of Stalin's Russia. In a sense it represented all the stored-up life chances of the Russians who were forced to make it, all the things they would have done with their time if they were not so compelled. One could look at it and see Stakhanovism, "socialist emulation," shock work, the infamous labor book that every worker had to carry, with his entire record in it, the entire Victorian system of labor relations that was in effect in Soviet industry, and this under the dictatorship of the proletariat. Could it have been made more cheaply, more efficiently, more humanely, more rationally, by hands other than those of Stalin? This is not a simple question to answer.

Should we at least agree with the Russian premise that it had to be made? And that we are delighted that, one way or another, it was made and helped save the world from Nazism? These are questions for students of history to discuss.

CHAPTER 14

A Debate: Was Stalin Necessary?

W e end this inquiry with a little debate. The topic, or rather the cluster of topics, has to do with the question of historical necessity. How much of the history discussed in this volume should be regarded as having been avoidable or, on the other side, fortuitous?

Not long after the end of the war, but before the death of Stalin, Isaac Deutscher, in what became a celebrated work, *Stalin: a Political Biography*, raised the question of whether Stalin had been "historically necessary." Deutscher offered the view that his subject should be separated from the literary context of twentieth-century wickedness where he stands as a peer of Hitler. Deutscher was at the time one of the most valued authorities on Soviet subjects, largely because of his ex-Communist credentials and his intimate knowledge of the international movement. As a member of the Polish Communist party, he had opposed Stalin's turn toward collectivization of agriculture in 1928, a critique that resulted in his expulsion. He and Trotsky, for different reasons, became exiles at about the same time.

Although he had been, strictly speaking, a supporter of the Bukharin position, when he read Trotsky's account of the rise of Stalin, he found himself in agreement. From this point on he was to champion Trotsky's line of anti-Stalinism, including the analysis found in Trotsky's *The Revolution Betrayed* of 1936. Deutscher, however, could not go along with Trotsky's notion of the political overthrow of the Stalinist "bureaucracy," nor that the Stalin leadership of the Comintern was entirely counter-revolutionary. He refused to join with Trotsky in the project of a Fourth International. That was a way of saying that Stalin, despite everything, still represented the Russian revolution, which was then spreading, as Deutscher saw it, to China and other countries. Deutscher was a kind of Trotskyist, but one who counted Stalin as a revolutionary, as he put it, one of the great line of "revolutionary despots."

Deutscher wanted to avoid the *grand guignol* imagery that customarily engulfs the subject of the Russian revolution. Not that there would be any point in attempting to slight the crimes of the Stalin era or their inevitable comparison with those of Nazism. One cannot deny the striking similarity of the Nazi and Soviet state regimes of the 1930s, with their ubiquitous police, their organized enthusiasm, their cult of the leader, their many victims. The technology available to twentieth-century dictatorships created many common features. Deutscher had to take note of these. Both Stalin and Hitler "built up the machinery of a totalitarian state," he wrote, "each striving to remold the mind of his nation in a single pattern, establishing himself as master in accordance with a rigid *führerprinzip.*"

Yet the ideas that drove those two regimes were completely different, as different as Karl Marx and Carl Schmitt. Communism was an offshoot of the multifaceted socialism of the nineteenth century that espoused an ideal according to which industrial society asserts in one way or another a public interest and claims a say in its future apart from the influence of the market. Fascism and Nazism were offshoots of the nineteenth-century ideal of racial supremacy, mobilizing science to achieve racial purity and imperial conquest without limit. The socialist ideal, however naively, tried to march in step with the social changes of the last two centuries; the fascist ideal was to turn them back. In the final analysis, Communism was the issue of revolution and Nazism of counterrevolution. While the regimes of Stalinism and Nazism were similar in their functions of police repression and terror, Communist doctrine could never take the regime as anything more than an expedient, a device. After Stalin's death, his successors immediately stopped the terror and tried to get back to a rational and legalist conception of rule. By contrast, Nazism in its worst excesses was entirely true to itself.

Taking note of these things, Deutscher's view ran sharply counter to a Western scholarly consensus of the first period of the Cold War that ended in the 1960s. Even after that, the debate on the comparison of Stalin and Hitler continued. Today one finds the discussion extended to include Islamism, perhaps in the thought that the ideological premises of the Cold War are still useful after its close. This is a lively discussion with which the student of the Russian revolution would have to be familiar. I have come to doubt the ability of the contestation to continue to produce insights, but this does not suggest that it can be ignored.

Rather than pursue the comparison of Hitler and Stalin according to the totalitarian model that he partially accepted, Deutscher preferred to compare Stalin with the revolutionary despots, Cromwell, Robespierre, and Napoleon. Like Cromwell, Stalin was present at the creation of the revolution and, playing different roles, including dictator, saw it through its various phases. Like Robespierre, he bled white his own party. Like Napoleon, "half conservative, half-revolutionary," he broke the back of the revolution at home while he advanced it abroad. Deutscher fell in with the received opinion of the 1930s that the Russian revolution could best be understood in terms of the English and French revolutions.

Historian Crane Brinton, in his *Anatomy of Revolution* (1938), had grouped all three revolutions into a common scheme including a radical "Jacobin" phase, Thermidor, Bonapartism, and Restoration. Brinton included a last phase of re-revolution after the Restoration, as with the "Glorious revolution" of 1689 and the French overthrow of the Bourbons in 1830, events that brought the great revolutions to a finish by ensuring that they would not be reversed. According to Brinton's picture we might expect some kind of Russian re-revolution in the future, some minimal restatement of Soviet ideals.

At the time of the fall of the Shah of Iran in 1979, there was a scramble in Washington to find copies of Brinton, in the hope that they might lend some perspectives from which to judge the Islamic revolution of Khomenei. This was a tribute to Brinton as a historian. Yet it has to be noted that Brinton had a difficult time with his categories, for example, in demonstrating the Russian Thermidor. As we have seen in Chapter 11, there have been many different dates suggested. Deutscher moreover claimed to locate a Bonapartist phase in the post-war expansion of Russian power into East Central Europe. Napoleon and Stalin both suppressed the revolution at home while they exported it abroad. Napoleon stopped the mass demonstration on the Champs de Mar with the famous "whiff of grapeshot." Stalin systematically murdered the Old Bolsheviks who had worked with Lenin. Napoleon and Stalin then took the revolution beyond its borders. Boris Yeltsin has certainly been the agent of a kind of restoration while, at the same time, at least in my opinion, also being an agent, with Gorbachev, of an 1848-style democratic revolution. Despite many suggestive comparisons and correspondences, it is still not easy to stamp Brinton's grid or any other on the history of the revolution.

Another alternative has been to see the Russian revolution as the revenge of timeless Russia. This view is constantly gaining adherents in post-Soviet Russia. It comes from Nikolai Berdyaev's suggestion that Stalinism was no more than "a new form of the hypertrophy of the state in Russian history." Western Marxism, according to Berdyaev, could not in itself have been capable of creating such a Leviathan. The forbear of Stalin was Peter the Great. Berdyaev said that "Peter's methods were purely Bolshevik." One can readily see that this is an intellectual point of least resistance for post-Soviet Russian nationalist speculation. The multinational Russian state needs an "ideology," or so say the nationalist, former Communist, Russian intellectuals, in their habitually Stalinist way. If it can no longer be Communism, they reason, it can only be the Russian Idea, the imperial Eurasian idea of the historical Russian state. This is the "Red-Brown" ideology of those who are reeling from the destruction of the Soviet Union and the recruitment of the former Soviet bloc into NATO.

Eurasianism is a Russian reflex. One of Boris Yeltsin's first foreign policy acts after liquidating the Soviet Union was to remind the world that Russia is a Eurasian power. Some Russian nationalist intellectuals see this as an imperative toward a "Eurasian" bloc with China, India, Iran, and others against "Atlanticism." This is expressed sanely, as a geopolitical reality in the light of NATO expansion, or deliriously, as a "red-brown" fantasy. Where Berdyaev once spoke of the line of continuity from the Third Rome to the Third International, fantastic enough when one thinks of it, one now hears ravings about a line from the Third Rome to the Third Reich to the Third International.

Russian ultranationalists have revived Stalin. Today's Russian Communists are as responsible as any others for this. They cleaned up some of the Stalinist mess in the glasnost period with their rehabilitation of most of the Old Bolsheviks, although, as George Orwell might have said, some were rehabilitated more than others. The "genuinely Russian" rightists such as Bukharin got a more thorough scrubbing than the "cosmopolitan" leftists, such as Radek, Zinoviev, and Trotsky. They were all posthumously cleared of the crimes charged to them in the Moscow Trials. But Gorbachev himself pronounced, in his 1987 speech on the 70th anniversary of the revolution, that Stalin had been right against all the oppositions and the bourgeois nationalists. So Russian Communism never got the cleansing and reshaping that Deutscher had hoped for. No wonder then that the post-Soviet Russian Communists settled on Stalin as the vehicle for their movement of national regeneration. Taking it a step further, the Russian ultranationalists have now produced a Stalin who is not a Communist, merely one

in a line of great Russian leaders, a kind of "demotic tsar," to borrow
the phrase of historian Robert Service.

Pursuing this thought from a different perspective, some have gone
so far as to see the Bolsheviks retrospectively as perpetrators of a xen-
ophobic Great Russian movement. This approach has a certain attrac-
tion for formerly subject non-Russian peoples, such as the Poles or the
Ukrainians. The material in these pages on National Bolshevism and
its many ramifications may seem to support this. Some who accept
Trotsky's analysis might see Stalin as a residue of nationalist mysticism
tout court. In the end, however, one must grant to Soviet Communism
its status as a Western idea, one which its founders recognized as
making no sense outside the context of a German revolution. Lenin
and Trotsky saw to it that the first meetings of the Comintern, housed
in Moscow, were conducted in German. For the Bolsheviks of the early
days, the German revolution would have made possible the great link
to Central European culture.

This link with Germany was viewed by occasionally sympathetic
non-Bolsheviks as producing something superior to Latin culture,
something outside the mainstream of liberal progressive thought.
The idea was represented in fiction by the odd charismatic character
Naphta, the Jewish Jesuit in Thomas Mann's *The Magic Mountain* of
1924, who expresses, in his invocation of a new medievalism, a new
organic collectivism coming out of the east, with the Communist proletariat the creator of a new religious unity: "its task is to strike terror
into the world for the healing of the world, that man may finally
achieve salvation and deliverance, and win back at length to freedom
from law and from distinction of classes, to his original status as a
child of God." Naphta's foil is his pompous but innocent friend
Settembrini, who defends a straightforward and radical reading of
the Western civic tradition, one which looks to the day "when thrones
would crash and outworn religions crumble, in those remaining countries of Europe which had not yet enjoyed the blessings of eighteenth
century enlightenment, not yet of an upheaval like 1789 ... it would
come if not on the wings of doves then on the pinions of eagles; and
dawn would break all over Europe, the dawn of universal brother-
hood, in the name of justice, science, and human reason."

Mann was writing after the world war about prewar cultural and
political expectations. He saw the war as hastening a general crisis of
civilization, with all the force of the progressive and revolutionary tradition bearing down on Central Europe and specifically the Habsburg
Empire, ready to wash away everything old and reactionary. Yet he
wondered if, in the wake of the catastrophe, the union of the German

and Russian cultures might produce something new and original undreamed of in the Italo-French Latinity of the Renaissance and the Enlightenment, whether the modern movement of Communism might promise the "triumph of man over economics" and some new organic link to tradition. "Are the Russian and the German attitudes toward Europe, western civilization, and politics not basically akin? Haven't we Germans also had our Slavophiles and westerners?"

In the end, however, Bolshevism should be probably seen as closer to Settembrini than to Naphta. The same Enlightenment that encouraged the elaborate and ambitious traditions of civil society inspired as well Communist universalism, which Russians call *obshchechelovechestvo*, universal human values. In its name Gorbachev tore apart the Soviet power. By 1990–1991 as the revolutions in the Soviet bloc spread into the Soviet Union, those who backed Gorbachev claimed the perspective of universal human values that they set against the line of Gorbachev's opponents, the line of class struggle. Nothing could demonstrate more clearly the persistence of Western notions of freedom at the core of the Soviet ideological outlook. Communism was originally a detour of Western socialism into the east and never stopped longing to come home.

Was Stalin necessary? The question that Deutscher raised was pursued through the decades of the Cold War mostly by Sovietologists, among them mostly by economists. It was a debate about whether the Five Year Plans were key to the defeat of the Nazis. But it was also a debate about the idea of rationality in planning. Economist and Sovietologist Alec Nove sounded the main themes. Stalin had completed the second phase of the industrialization of the country, the first having been completed in the 1890s through the leadership of Count Witte. Every kind of inefficiency could be found in the economic methods of the dictatorship, and alternatives could have been found to the ways of collectivization of agriculture. But in the end industrialization and modernization had to be pursued, however untidy the process. Stalin did, despite everything, accomplish this.

One can imagine Lenin, Bukharin, and Stalin debating these issues in a didactic play like Mikhail Shatrov's *Forward, Forward, Forward,* of which Russians are so fond. Even if a Lenin or Stalin character appears to win the point above, someone else on stage would counter that the makers of the October revolution never had the slightest intention of modernizing Russia when they took power in 1917. They modernized to prepare the country to confront Britain and France, their eventual allies. At the start in 1927 they hoped that Germany would be with them. Must we then thank them for putting the country through everything it suffered between 1927 and 1941 in order to win a victory in a struggle they did not and could not have foreseen? No good answer is possible to this, unless one is content to invoke Hegel's Cunning of Reason, according to which we cannot know the real consequences of our decisions. In Bismarck's famous figure, God sweeps by us and we try desperately to clutch at his garment.

Nove held that the purges of 1936–1938, however, were a detour and added to the difficulty. If the discussion was an exercise in divining rationality in the Soviet system of planning and command, the purges, especially the military purge, were the height of irrationality. This was accepted by Khrushchëv in the secret speech of 1956 and revived in the glasnost literature at the end the 1980s. A dissenting voice, that of V. M. Molotov, maintained that the purges had been a way to stop a fifth column from aiding a future invader. Molotov, in his memoirs, gave the example of the French defeat in 1940 and argued that because of the purges he and Stalin had made sure that there was no fifth column to aid Hitler: an argument from military necessity. To accept it, you have to assume that Stalin and Molotov wanted above all to prepare to fight the Nazis and that the Nazi-Soviet pact of 1939 was only a way of buying time before the inevitable struggle with the bestial enemy.

The "fifth column" argument and "buying time" were advanced as a pair. The preceding chapters have for the most part rejected this in favor of the "war avoidance" theme. Stalin and Molotov were not buying time; the 1939 pact only made sense as part of a strategy to stay out of the war altogether. If one considers the purges as a way to get free of those such as Bukharin who would have objected to the pact, the argument becomes one for the the purges as war avoidance. So here are two different arguments for the "rationality" of the irrational purges. It is surprising to me how much Molotov's argument from the fifth column threat is accepted by historians, including those who had done research in Soviet archives. You have to imagine the Old Bolsheviks eager to make common cause with the Nazis, just as it is described in the Moscow Trials.

The economic debate followed Deutscher's lines of thought. Moreover, it took up the idea of a Stalinist modernization model for an agrarian country. This might apply to the Communist regimes in North Korea, Cuba, and other places, or the countries in Africa and Asia presumably undergoing what the Soviets then called "non-capitalist development." This is no longer a hot topic. No one today talks about non-capitalist development in Africa and Asia. Quite the reverse; one talks about the transition to closer connection to the world market. Yet for a time there was a kind of acceptance, grudging or not, among economists such as Alexander Gerschenkron and Gregory Grossman, and historians such as Theodore Von Laue, that the Soviet model, despite its distortions, did steer rapid modernization and, moreover, provided, along with a stifling and only semi-rational dictatorship, a welfare state that improved its services right up to the Gorbachev era.

Western socialists might find this endorsement, such as it was, rather cold-blooded. Was Stalin necessary to build a socialist state? To admit this would be impossible. Stalinism is something for socialism to live down. The Soviets tried to live it down during the rule of Khrushchev and Gorbachev and finally ended socialism in the process. It might well be said that Stalin set the socialist idea back more than any of its opponents. To the suggestion that it was an aberration, there is the inevitable retort that socialism is as socialism does. Big government is not the solution but the problem. How to contend with the forceful citation of the Soviet experience as a caution even against the progress of the welfare state? Does one opt for a road to serfdom when one urges a Western state to build schools and hospitals, to exact a progressive income tax, to provide a legal basis for trade unions? Certainly one has to draw a line between Soviet and Western ideas of socialism.

At the least, one must recognize the special historical circumstances that gave rise to Stalinism in Russia. As argued earlier in these pages, the revolution was originally a mutiny. Unless one demonstrates the outstanding virtue of World War I, one cannot consider this mutiny to be the apex of wickedness. The Russian people, thus embarked, found that they could not get out of the war without the Bolsheviks. The Constituent Assembly of 1918 would probably have kept them in the war, as Kerensky tried to do, and as the Whites thereafter also strove to do. If any of these people had got Russia back into the war, it would have finished even more raggedly than it did with the Bolsheviks. The cities would have been depopulated without the Communists and their compulsory grain requisitions. The country would have been a sort of bedraggled, disintegrating Weimar Russia.

Everything in the shaping of the Communist regime in Russia seems to have been forced. Only under the circumstances of the civil war and allied intervention can one imagine the anarchistic revolution submitting to the leadership of the Bolsheviks. War Communism shaped and defined the dictatorship. No wonder that War Communism returned in the form of the Stalinist Big Drive, collectivizing agriculture and decreeing planned economy. Was Stalin necessary for this? He was certainly an able leader in the civil war. But so were the other Bolsheviks. Stalin was not indispensable in the sense that Lenin and Trotsky, or other Bolsheviks, or a collective leadership with Stalin in a lesser role, could not have done what he did. War Communism would have been second nature to any of them. The alternative to the quite unnecessary Stalin could have directed a regime of permanent War Communism at least as well as he, without a permanent bacchanalia of murder and denunciation. Was Stalin the only one to lead the unfortunate Russian revolution to victory?

Putting this another way, could Stalin have led this victory without the revolution? One might think so, to read the Russian ultranationalists, who imagine him on horseback, shouting "Na Rus" and waving on the Russian hordes against the Teutonic Knights. This is all nonsense, of course. Stalin could lead the country to victory only by blending nationalism with the passions and energies of the revolution. Was Russian nationalism necessary? Probably. Was the revolution necessary? Probably. A military dictatorship by Kornilov or some other White general could never have industrialized the country. At its best, it would have been in the condition of Poland in 1939, easy pickings for the Nazis. A multiparty democracy, perhaps a state led by the Socialist Revolutionary party, would have been more recognizable to Western progressives. It would have had a vigorous socialist opposition as did most European states. But what happened to them? When populists wore out their welcome the right rose up in Bulgaria in 1923, in Poland in 1926, eventually in every state in East Central Europe, save the admirable Czechoslovakia, which today no longer exists. These were easy pickings for the Nazis, as Russia would also have been.

Was the Russian revolution necessary? Could the Nazis have been defeated some other way? This is a bit like asking whether the United States could have played its role in the world wars if Lincoln had not won the civil war. It is hard to imagine getting along without Lincoln. We are merely saying that one big event made possible another big event. So the whole world, certainly the Atlantic world, can be said to have found a real friend in the Russian revolution in World War II. This was the attitude of Churchill and Roosevelt. Hitler and Mussolini had done everything in their power to convince them that their true interests lay with anti-Communism, but they would not listen. Despite all the formidable issues that divided the main actors of the anti-fascist coalition, history, and this includes time and chance, brought about their unity. It was, in a way, the unity of all their revolutions, the English revolution, the French revolution, the American, and the Russian. These are the main revolutions in the tradition of Western civilization; that is, they are the landmarks of its major leaps in institutional progress. It is bizarre to think that Stalin, this monster, this devil, this champion of mass murder, this ignorant stifler of the creative impulses of a mighty, brilliant people, led the Russian revolution in its greatest victory, and that this was such a great victory for the world. It is a terrible, ridiculous irony, but perhaps not a tragedy.

In any case, we now say good-bye to the Russian revolution. It leaves us with a mixed picture. Those who think seriously about it will come to various conclusions. It would be a good thing if one could resist the temptation to think of it as a unique example of the devil's work on earth, even if aspects of it are certainly devilish. Instead it would be better to think of it as a historical phenomenon in a special setting at a special time—not merely a cautionary tale or a horror story to be told over a campfire, but something worthy of study by every thinking human.

Suggestions for Further Reading

CHAPTER 1

Bernard Pares was the leading British expert on Russia during the period covered by this volume. Director of the University of London's School of Slavonic Studies and editor of *Slavonic and East European Review*, he was a former British officer on the Russian front in World War I and liaison to Kolchak's White government during the civil war. He examines the Russian character, with a breathless inventory of Russia's resources, in *Russia* (New York, Mentor, 1943). Older attempts at the same task, still readable and stimulating, are Anatole Leroy-Beaulieu, *The Empire of the Tsars and the Russians* (New York and London, 1893) and Paul Miliukov, *Outlines of Russian Culture* (Philadelphia, 1948). Bertram Wolfe provides a lyrical description of the setting of modern Russian history in a chapter, "The Heritage," from his classic, *Three Who Made a Revolution* (Boston, 1948). Wolfe was a Communist in the 1920s, a supporter of the right when Bukharin was prominent in the Bolshevik leadership. He later broke with Communism, writing widely and eloquently on related subjects. Aleksandr Blok's "Scythians" is in Robert Goldwin (ed.), *Readings in Russian Foreign Policy* (Oxford, 1959). Polish counterpoint to the above is available through Henryk Paszkiewicz, *The Origins of Russia* (New York, 1954). For the Ukrainian view, a cogent brief statement is given by Ivan Rudnytsky, "The Role of the Ukraine in Modern Society," in Donald Treadgold (ed.), *The Development of the USSR: An Exchange of Views* (Seattle, 1964). An essay stressing discontinuities between Kiev and Muscovy is Marshall Poe, *The Russian Moment in World History* (Princeton and Oxford, 2003). George Vernadsky's *Ancient Russia* (New Haven, 1943) puts the emphasis on Eurasian themes. It can be compared with P. M. Barford, *The Early Slavs: Culture and Society in Early Medieval Eastern Europe* (Ithaca, 2001). Religious philosopher Nicolas Berdyaev stresses the peculiarities of the Russian religious experience in *The Origin of Russian Communism* (New York, 1937). Berdyaev was a Marxist at the turn of the century who converted to Orthodoxy in 1905. Nevertheless he supported the revolution and taught at Moscow until 1922, when he left his academic post for Berlin and later Paris. His ideas enjoyed a revival with the glasnost campaign in 1987. Richard Pipes's eloquent and rigorous essay on the concept of the social diarchy is in his introduction to *Karamzin's Memoir on Ancient and Modern Russia* (Cambridge, 1959). The tsardom as the salvation of the nation is the central idea of S. F. Platonov, *Moscow and the West* (Academic International, 1972). A more ironic version of the same argument is Voltaire, *Russia under Peter the Great* (London and Toronto, 1983).

CHAPTER 2

An array of provocative essays on the intelligentsia may be found in Richard Pipes (ed.), *The Russian Intelligentsia* (New York, 1961). Philip Pomper, *The Russian Revolutionary Intelligentsia* (New York, 1970) is a concise survey. One can also consult Daniel Brower, "The Problem of the Intelligentsia," *Slavic Review* (December 1967). Donald Mackenzie Wallace, *Russia* (New York, 1877), is a fascinating contemporary essay by a sophisticated British journalist. More recent accounts include Andrei Sinyavsky, *The Russian Intelligentsia* (New York, 1997), with sharp observations from a famous *samizdat* critic of the Soviet regime, and Vladimir Nahirny, *The Russian Intelligentsia: From Torment to Silence* (New Brunswick, 1983). Radishchev, Novikov, and Fonvizin, the first critics of serfdom in the era of Catherine the Great, are discussed in Hans Rogger, *National Consciousness in Eighteenth Century Russia* (Cambridge, 1960). For the Decembrists, see Krista Agnew, "The French Revolutionary Influence on the Russian Decembrists," *Consortium on Revolutionary Europe*, 22 (1993). Martin Malia, *Alexander Herzen and the Birth of Russian Socialism* (Cambridge, 1961), tracing Herzen's intellectual evolution through various phases, including anarchism at the end, was considered a model of how to write intellectual history when the genre was most in vogue. Franco Venturi, *Roots of Revolution* (New York, 1960), is a still unsurpassed classic on Populism. Avrahm Yarmolinsky's *Road to Revolution* (London, 1957) is slightly more accessible. Yarmolinsky is scathing on the "movements to the people," for him examples of "children's crusade." For the bourgeoisie and civil society, there are superb essays in Edith Clowes, Samuel Kassow, and James West (eds.), *Between Tsar and People* (Princeton, 1991). Orlando Figes, *Natasha's Dance* (London, 2002), stresses the social and cultural intimacy between the intelligentsia and the peasantry. Feodor Dostoyevsky's ruminations on the Eastern Question are in "Geok-Tepe: What Is Asia to Us?" in *Diary of a Writer*, trans. Boris Brasol (New York, 1949).

CHAPTER 3

An overview of the regime's modernization problems can be found in Peter Gatrell, "Modernization Strategies and Outcomes in Pre-Revolutionary Russia," in Markku Kangaspuro and Jeremy Smith (eds.), *Modernization in Russia since 1900* (Helsinki, 2006). Hans Rogger, *Russia in the Age of Modernization and Revolution, 1881–1917* (London and New York, 1983), centers on the problem of the relationship of state to society in the context of Russia's role as a great power and multinational empire. Roberta Manning, *The Crisis of the Old Order in Russia* (Princeton, 1982) puts the stress on the gentry and its defense of class interests. Tim McDaniel, *Autocracy, Capitalism, and Revolution in Russia* (Berkeley, Los Angeles and London, 1988), offers the model of a presumably doomed "autocratic capitalism." The best place to review tsarist foreign policy is Barbara Jelavich, *A Century of Russian Foreign Policy, 1814–1914* (Philadelphia and New York, 1964). The works of Charles and Barbara Jelavich, who were my teachers, are useful on Russia and the Balkans. George Kennan, *The Decline of Bismarck's European Order: Franco-Russian Relations, 1875–1890* (Princeton, 1979), taking the Franco-Russian alliance to be inevitable, is an attempt to counter the more established view of the most distinguished diplomatic historians, such as William L. Langer, *The Franco-Russian Alliance, 1890–1894* (Cambridge, 1929), who considered it irrational in the extreme. David McDonald, *Unified Government and Foreign Policy in Russia, 1900–1914* (Cambridge, MA, 1992), explores the struggle for control between the autocrat and his ministers. On industrialization, there is Theodore Von Laue, *Sergei Witte and the Industrialization of Russia* (New York, 1963), an exercise in the cultural slope argument in Chapter 2, which is continued in Von Laue's other works, e.g., *Why Lenin? Why Stalin?* (Philadelphia, 1971). He calls Russia a power "on credit only." The classic study of the peasantry is Geroid Robinson, *Rural Russia under the Old Regime* (Berkeley and Los Angeles, 1967) in which the momentum of agrarian revolution is inexorable. Leopold Haimson's influential article, "The Problem of

Social Stability in Urban Russia," *Slavic Review* (December 1964 and March 1965) says something similar about the urban workers. For the workers, see Reginald Zelnik, *A Radical Worker in Tsarist Russia* (Stanford, 1986) and Victoria Bonnell, *Roots of Rebellion: Workers' Politics and Organization in Saint Petersburg and Moscow, 1900–1914* (Berkeley and Los Angeles, 1984). Claudie Weill, *Marxistes russes et social-democratie allemande, 1898–1904* (Paris, 1977), has the best discussion of the Mensheviks' unsuccessful appeal to the German Socialists to drum Bolshevism out of the International. L. D. Trotsky, *1905*, trans. Anya Bostok, (New York, 1971), is informative. Richard Pipes, *Struve: Liberal on the Right, 1905–1944* (Cambridge, MA, 1980), a biography on a grand scale, should be compared with Martin Malia's biography of Herzen, cited in Chapter 2. Jacob Walkin, in *The Rise of Democracy in Pre-Revolutionary Russia* (New York, 1962), makes an eloquent case for the position of V. N. Maklakov that the liberals should have cooperated with the best of the tsarist bureaucrats. Geoffrey Hosking, *The Russian Constitutional Experiment and Duma, 1907–1914* (Cambridge University Press, 1973), examines the tense relations between the Octobrists and Stolypin in the last two Dumas.

CHAPTER 4

Two older studies of the last acts of the tsarist order are still useful: Michael Florinsky, *The End of the Russian Empire* (New York, 1931), and Bernard Pares, *The Fall of the Russian Monarchy* (London and New York, 1939). Durnovo's warnings and previsions can be consulted in P. N. Durnovo, "Memorandum to Nicholas the Second," in Thomas Riha (ed.), *Readings in Russian Civilization*, vol. 2 (Chicago and London, 1964). For the borderlands of the empire, there is Derek Spring, "Russian Imperialism in Asia in 1914," *Cahiers du Monde Russe et Soviétique* (July–December, 1979). Allan Wildman, *The End of the Russian Imperial Army* (Princeton, 1980), examines the breakdown of military discipline and the role of the soldiers' committees. Norman Stone, *The Eastern Front, 1914–1917* (London and New York, 1975) sees the mobilization as in effect one for war and revolution at the same time. F. L. Carsten, *War against War* (Berkeley and Los Angeles, 1982), is a study of the international movement against the war. Jules Humbert-Droz, *L'Origine de l'internationale Communiste* (Paris, 1968), does the same with a focus on the Zimmerwald and Kienthal conferences. Georges Haupt, *Socialism and the Great War* (Oxford, 1972) holds Karl Kautsky's theory of

ultra-imperialism responsible for the fact that the war was not antici-
pated. Kautsky's idea describes more or less what is implied by
neo-liberalism today. For Rosa Luxemburg and her views about
Bolshevism, see the large-scale biography, J. P. Nettl, *Rosa Luxemburg*
(London, 1966).

CHAPTER 5

The literature on the year 1917 is vast, as with other topics discussed in these pages. There are many interpretations, almost all of
which illuminate some side of the historical issues. The student might
do best by plunging into original documents and firsthand accounts;
some of the latter have risen to the level of notable literature of the
twentieth century. For documents, there is Mark Steinberg, *Voices of
the Revolution, 1917* (New Haven and London, 2001), in the Yale
University Press Annals of Communism series, with many newly translated letters and circulars. As for personal accounts, N. N. Sukhanov,
The Russian Revolution, 1917: A Personal Record (Princeton, 1984),
gives a Menshevik perspective. Often overlooked, it is full of detail and
shrewd observation. One gap is the Bolshevik meeting of October 10,
which was held at his apartment; his wife, a Bolshevik, neglected to
inform him. Alexander Kerensky, *The Crucifixion of Liberty* (New
York, 1972), explicates his impossible position with eloquence. Leon
Trotsky, *The Russian Revolution*, 3 vols., (London, 1967) is at least as
accurate a guide to the revolution as Winston Churchill's volumes are
to World War II, and in the same category of towering rhetorical literature. It is most informative at the beginning and, oddly, most diffuse at
the end. John Reed, *Ten Days That Shook the World* (Middlesex and
New York, 1982), captures the atmosphere of the mass meetings. The
most reliable account of affairs in the capital is Alexander Rabinowitch,
The Bolsheviks Come to Power (New York, 1976), augmented by his
later writings. Just as good, with a different scope, is Robert Daniels,
Red October (New York, 1967). Roy Medvedev, *The October Revolution* (New York, 1979), falls short of this high standard, despite its keen
knowledge of most issues, because of a certain Lenin cultishness. There
are many studies of a slightly more specialized character. The breakdown
of the Russian army is described in Allan Wildman, *The Road to Soviet
Power and Peace* (Princeton, 1987), the latter of his two volumes on
the subject. Oliver Radkey, *Agrarian Foes of Bolshevism* (New York,
1958), is by the historian of the SR party, which, had there been no
war, would probably have ruled, no doubt with crises like that of
Poland's peasant party. The problems of the Kadets and Octobrists are

surveyed in William Rosenberg, *The Liberals in the Russian Revolution* (Princeton, 1974). For the Mensheviks, there is Abraham Ascher (ed.), *The Mensheviks in the Russian Revolution* (Ithaca, 1976). For the anarchists, see Anthony D'Agostino, "Anarchists in 1917," in George Jackson (ed.), *Dictionary of the Russian Revolution* (New York, Westport, and London, 1989). For the gentry, one can consult Matthew Rendle, "Symbolic Revolution: The Russian Nobility and February 1917," *Revolutionary Russia*, vol. 1 (2005). The workers have got a good deal of attention in useful works, among which are David Mandel, *The Petrograd Workers and the Soviet Seizure of Power* (London, 1984); William Rosenberg and Diane Koenker, *Strikes and Revolution in Russia, 1917* (Princeton, 1988); Mary McAuley, *Bread and Justice: State and Society in Petrograd* (New York and Oxford, 1991); and Steven Smith, *Red Petrograd: Revolution in the Factories, 1917–1918* (Cambridge, 1983). For the rising of the Kazakh and Kirghiz peoples in Central Asia see Edward Sokol, *The Revolt of 1916 in Central Asia* (Baltimore, 1954).

CHAPTER 6

For half a century the most reliable guide to the civil war in all its aspects was William Henry Chamberlain, *The Russian Revolution*, vol. 2, *From the Civil War to the Consolidation of Power* (London, 1935). Now there is Ewan Mawdsley, *The Russian Civil War* (Boston and London, 1987). The passages from the Manifesto of the Communist International are in Alix Holt, Barbara Holland, and Alan Adler (eds.), *Theses, Resolutions, and Manifestoes of the First Four Congresses of the Third International* (London, 1980). Lars Lih, *Bread and Authority in Russia, 1914–1921* (Berkeley and Los Angeles, 1990), and "Our Position Is in the Highest Degree Tragic: Bolshevik 'Euphoria' in 1920," in Mike Haynes and Jim Wolfreys (eds.), *History and Revolution* (London and New York, 2007), put the forced nature of the Bolshevik evolution into sharp relief. Victor Serge, *Memoirs of a Revolutionary* (London and Oxford, 1963), records the impressions of an anarchist who made an uneasy peace with Bolshevism. Geoffrey Swain, *The Origins of the Russian Civil War* (London and New York, 1996), makes the case for the "Green Revolution" of the SRs and others who spoke for the democracy of 1917 and the Constituent Assembly against the Bolsheviks. Peter Kenez, *The Civil War in South Russia*, 2 vols., (Berkeley and Stanford, 1971, 1977) details the mistakes of the White leaders. For the foreign policy of the Soviet state, as distinct from its Comintern policy, see Richard Debo, *Survival and*

Consolidation: The Foreign Policy of Soviet Russia, 1918–1921 (Montreal, 1992). The British service to Russia in defeating Imperial Germany is described in Brian Pearce, *How Haig Saved Lenin* (Basingstoke, 1987). On the allied intervention, one still has to start with George Kennan, *Soviet-American Relations, 1917–1920*, 2 vols. (Princeton, 1956, 1958). David Fogelsong, *America's Secret War against Bolshevism: U.S. Intervention in the Russian Civil War–1920* (Chapel Hill, 1995) argues that U.S. policy followed in Russia the model of the Mexican intervention of 1914 and was not confused or contradictory, as it certainly seems, but secret. This argument requires deemphasis of the policy of the other powers. For Britain, there is Richard Ullman, *Anglo-Soviet Relations, 1917–1921*, 3 vols. (Princeton, 1961–1972). For France, see Michael Carley, *Revolution and Intervention: The French Government and the Russian Civil War* (Kingston, 1983), tracing policy controversies and widespread French activities. Piotr Wandycz, *Soviet-Polish Relations, 1917–1921* (Harvard, 1969), tells the story of Poland's struggle for great power status and the conflicts between its ambitious soldier, Piłsudski, and his nemesis Roman Dmowski, who wanted to stay on good terms with Russia. A detailed study of the Kronstadt sailors' version of Soviet power without political parties is Israel Getzler, *Kronstadt, 1917–1921: Fate of a Soviet Democracy* (Cambridge, 1983), by the sympathetic biographer of Martov.

CHAPTER 7

Historical works on the rise of Stalin originally observed the etiquette of the dispute between Stalin's Socialism in One Country and Trotsky's Permanent Revolution. Trotsky's own version was followed by Isaac Deutscher and, after him, E. H. Carr. The most lucid rendering of the interpretation is in Isaac Deutscher, *The Prophet Unarmed: Trotsky, 1921–1929* (London, 1959). Robert Daniels, *Conscience of the Revolution* (Cambridge, 1960), augments this view slightly by noting a tendency toward totalitarianism from Lenin to Stalin. This continues to be a common theme, for example, in Robert Service, *The Iron Ring* (Bloomington, 1995), where Lenin, despite his attempts to contain both Trotsky and Stalin, is seen as the demiurge of a perfected totalitarianism. Stephen Cohen, *Bukharin and the Bolshevik Revolution* (New York, 1979), broke with the Stalin-Trotsky crux by suggesting that the main alternative to Stalin was not Trotsky but Bukharin and right Communism. Anthony D'Agostino, *Soviet Succession Struggles* (Boston and London, 1988), has Stalin and Trotsky as centrists with Zinoviev and Bukharin as the Leningrad left and the Moscow right, respectively. Richard B. Day's *Leon Trotsky and the Politics of Economic Isolation* (Cambridge, 1973) argues that Trotsky's real concern through-out was integration of the Soviet Union into the world economy. Michael Reiman, *The Birth of Stalinism* (Bloomington, 1987), focusing on the crisis of NEP, asserts that Stalin took virtually all his ideas from others. For him the 1927–1929 period is a crisis of NEP. For Mark von Hagen, *Soldiers in the Proletarian Dictatorship: The Red Army in the Soviet Socialist State, 1917–1930* (Ithaca, 1990), the army was the key to Stalin's rise, the collectivization of agriculture a return to War Communism. Terry Martin, *The Affirmative Action Empire: Nations and Nationalism in the Soviet Union, 1923–1939* (Ithaca, 2001), salutes the nuanced Soviet handling of the nationalities in a "post-imperialist" state. Nikolai Ustrialov's views about Soviet National Bolshevism are described in Mikhail Agursky, *The Third Rome: National Bolshevism in the Soviet Union* (Boulder, 1987), an approximate translation of the author's *Ideologiia natsional bol'shevizma*. Albert Mathiez's view of Bolshevik "Jacobinism" is in *Le Bolshevisme et le jacobinisme* (Bologna, 1920). In the last years of the Soviet regime, western historical studies focused on Soviet society rather than politics. The works of Sheila Fitz-patrick led the way, for example, *The Commissariat of Enlightenment: Soviet Organization of Education and the Arts under Lunacharsky* (Cambridge, 1970). The semi-radicalism of Soviet ideas about culture is investigated by Lynn Mally in *The Culture of the Future: The Proletkult Movement in Revolutionary Russia* (Berkeley, 1990). Peter Kenez, *The Birth of the Propaganda State: Soviet Methods of Mass Mobilization* (Cambridge, 1985), traces the views of leaders and the limits of their efforts. Aleksandra Kollontai, member of the Workers' Opposition in 1920, Commissar of Public Health, diplo-mat, socialist feminist, and later Stalinist diplomat, is appreciated in Beatrice Farnsworth, *Aleksandra Kollontai: Socialism, Feminism, and the Bolshevik Revolution* (Stanford, 1980). The quotation of Victor Serge is from his *Memoirs of a Revolutionary* (London and Oxford, 1963), 85.

CHAPTER 8

For many years the most reliable source for information about early Communist foreign policy was Louis Fischer, *The Soviets in World Affairs*, 2 vols. (Princeton, 1951). Fischer knew many prominent Soviet diplomats and went along with the idea that foreign policy had nothing to do with the activities of the Communist International.

Now there is Jon Jacobson, *When the Soviet Union Entered World Politics* (Berkeley, 1994), a work of broad synthesis and the best over-all guide to the topic. George Kennan, *Russia and the West under Lenin and Stalin* (Boston, 1961), was also for a long while a highly influential and lucid study depending for the most part on Fischer. Along with Franz Borkenau, *World Communism* (New York, 1929), it was a valuable education for sophisticated readers in the 1960s and 1970s. Succeeding generations looking deeper into the history would find Albert Lindemann, *Red Years: European Socialism versus Bolshevism, 1919–1921* (Berkeley, 1974) to be indispensable. A use-ful general survey is Teddy Uldricks, *Diplomacy and Ideology, 1917–1930* (London, 1979). An essay on anti-imperial themes is Ken Post, *Revolution's Other World: Communism and the Periphery, 1917–1939* (Basingstoke, 1997). As already indicated, the best place to consider Nikolai Ustrialov's theory of National Bolshevism is Mikhail Agursky, *The Third Rome: National Bolshevism in the Soviet Union* (Boulder, 1987), a translation and re-editing of the author's *Ideologiia national-bol'shevizma*. Robert Wohl, *French Communism in the Making, 1914–1924* (Stanford, 1966), covers a good deal more than the title indicates, including the international setting of the "Zinovievite Bolshevization" of the Comintern that drove out Boris Souvarine, later a pioneering Stalin biographer and Kremlinologist. The extraordinary story of M. N. Roy and the formation of the Mexican and Indian parties is told by Samaren Roy, *Twice-Born Heretic: M. N. Roy and the Comintern* (Calcutta, 1986). For the early attempts of Bolsheviks to get trade, credits, and recognition, there is Carole Fink, *Genoa, Rapallo, and the European Reconstruction in 1922* (Washington, 1991); and Steven White, *The Origins of Détente* (Berkeley, 1985). On the German October, there is Werner Angress, *Stillborn Revolution: The Communist Bid for Power in Germany, 1921–1923* (Princeton, 1963), making use of E. H. Carr's writings for the Soviet side, and the compendious Pierre Broué, *Révolution en allemagne, 1917–23* (Paris, 1971). The Canadian historian of Soviet foreign policy, Richard Debo, wrote his dissertation on Chicherin. One can access his views in "G. V. Chicherin: A Historical Perspec-tive," in Gabriel Gorodetsky (ed.), *Soviet Foreign Policy, 1917–1991: A Retrospective* (London, 1994). A current survey of the whole topic is Jonathan Haslam, "The Communist International and Soviet Foreign Policy," in Ronald Suny (ed.), *Cambridge History of Russia*, vol. 3 (Cambridge, 2006). On the Chinese revolution, see Conrad Brandt, *Stalin's Failure in China, 1924–1927* (New York, 1958). For the effects of the British general strike on British policy, see

Gabriel Gorodetsky, *The Precarious Truce: Anglo-Soviet Relations, 1924–1927* (Cambridge, 1977).

CHAPTER 9

The struggle among the Soviet leaders over economic alternatives in the 1920s may be followed in Alexander Ehrlich, *The Soviet Industrialization Debate* (Cambridge, Harvard University Press, 1960), which set the tone for subsequent literature on the rise of Stalin and interest in the Bukharin alternative. R. W. Davies, *The Socialist Offensive: Collectivization of Soviet Agriculture, 1929–1930* (London, Macmillan, 1980) looks closely at the problems and dilemmas of planned economy. It can be compared with the older, more categorically critical view of Noam Jasny, *Soviet Industrialization, 1928–1952* (Chicago, 1961). For collectivization, see V. P. Danilov, *Rural Russia under the New Regime* (Bloomington, 1988), a translated work by a leading Soviet historian concerned with the tragedy of collectivization and Bukharin's case against it, without giving an endorsement. The protracted chaos, the ruthlessness, and one-sided industrial mania of the period are described and explored in Moshe Lewin, *Russian Peasants and Soviet Power* (Evanston, IL, 1968), and Sheila Fitzpatrick, *Stalin's Peasants* (New York and Oxford, 1994). Lynne Viola, *Collectivization and the Culture of Peasant Resistance* (New York, 1996), tells the story of the vast peasant revolt against collectivization, considered as the greatest internal struggle against Soviet power. Louis Siegelbaum, *Stakhanovism and the Politics of Productivity in the USSR, 1935–1941* (Cambridge, 1988), looks closely at the coal industry and considers socialist emulation and its shortcomings as a recourse for the regime prior to a turn toward terror. Mark Tauger, "The 1932 Harvest and Famine of 1933," *Slavic Review* (Spring 1991), makes a modest and sensible addition to the debate over charges of genocide in the Ukraine. For a celebration of the victories of the campaign by a future celebrant of similar victories in Maoist China, see Anna Louise Strong, *The Soviets Conquer Wheat* (New York, Henry Holt, 1931). Stephen Kotkin, *The Magnetic Mountain: Stalinism as a Civilization* (Berkeley and Los Angeles, 1995) goes to Magnitogorsk to study the appeal to the workers of Soviet ideology and its version of a despotic welfare state. It can be compared with the earlier account of the same subject from the inside, John Scott, *Behind the Urals* (Cambridge MA, 1942). Kendall Bayles, *Technology and Society under Lenin and Stalin* (Princeton, 1978) is a study of the new intelligentsia of white-collar workers and professionals as a class.

CHAPTER 10

The literature of the Purge is vast and growing. It is a minefield of conflicting interpretations, rich in subtexts. Many facts are disputed and some views are based on more recently available documentary material than others. Not all the evidence speaks for itself. While it was all going on, the best information for the outside world was two émigré periodicals, the Menshevik *Socialist Courier* and the Trotskyist *Bulletin of the Opposition*. Boris Nikolaevsky, *Power and the Soviet Elite* (Ann Arbor, 1975), contains the famous "Letter of an Old Bolshevik" from a Nikolaevsky interview with Bukharin. The transcript of Trotsky's self-defense in English in several days of testimony is in Preliminary Commission of Inquiry, *The Case of Leon Trotsky* (New York, 1968). It is good to read these before the academic literature. Robert Conquest is the historian who has been the main point of reference, drawing on the Nikolaevsky material. *The Great Terror: A Reassessment* (New York, 1990) is the latest version of his work. He was challenged by J. Arch Getty, *Origins of the Great Purges: The Soviet Communist Party Reconsidered* (Cambridge, 1985) and subsequent works. Robert Thurston, *Life and Terror in Stalin's Russia, 1934–1941* (New Haven and London, 1996) took the Getty challenge a step further. Oleg Khlevniuk, *Master of the House: Stalin and His Inner Circle* (New Haven and London, 2009), using Soviet archival material, disputes Nikolaevsky and Getty. For the Comintern, see William Chase, *Enemies within the Gates? The Comintern and the Stalinist Repression, 1934–1939* (New Haven, 2001). Archival evidence for purge figures may be found in Anne Applebaum, *Gulag: A History* (Harmondsworth, 2004). Felix Chuev and Albert Resis (eds.), *Molotov Remembers* (Chicago, 1993), is taken seriously by all, as is Lars Lih, Oleg Naumov, and Oleg Khlevniuk (eds.), *Stalin's Letters to Molotov, 1925–1936* (New Haven, 1995).

CHAPTER 11

From the many volumes expressing disillusionment with the revolution, a few will indicate the main lines of interpretation. The story of the persecution of the anarchists and their case against Bolshevism is told in fullest detail by G. P. Maksimoff, *The Guillotine at Work: Twenty Years of Terror in Russia* (Chicago, 1940). For the Mensheviks in exile, there is a superb intellectual history, with a sort of key to Soviet politics, in André Liebich, *From the Other Shore: Russian Social Democracy after 1921* (Cambridge, MA, 1997). Ruth Fischer,

Stalin and German Communism: A Study in the Origins of the State Party (Cambridge, MA, 1948), speaking from the standpoint of Zinoviev's international faction, finds Soviet "National Bolshevism" the source of the problem. Trotsky's views may be found in many volumes of journalism and in *The Revolution Betrayed* (New York, 1937). For the second five-year plan as a "great retreat," see Nicholas Timasheff, *The Great Retreat* (New York, 1946), by a student of Russian religion and law, an interpretation influential in the 1950s and 1960s. Its view is more or less endorsed by Sheila Fitzpatrick, *The Russian Revolution* (Oxford and New York, 1994). For bureaucratic collectivism, there is Bruno Rizzi, *The Bureaucratization of the World: The USSR: Bureaucratic Collectivism* (London, 1985), a translation of his 1939 work with a thoughtful introduction by Adam Westoby. One offshoot of Rizzi was James Burnham, *The Managerial Revolution: What Is Happening in the World?* (New York, 1941). Burnham should be read with George Orwell's scathing critique, *James Burnham and the Managerial Revolution* (London, 1946), a pamphlet available in some libraries and easily searched on the Internet. The most sophisticated version of "bureaucratic collectivism" is in Max Shachtman, *The Bureaucratic Revolution* (New York, 1962), by a close associate of Trotsky who broke with him by means of this theory. A later, more simplified idea is in Milovan Djilas, *The New Class: An Analysis of the Communist System* (New York, 1957). In the same family is Mikhail Voslensky, *Nomenklatura: Anatomy of the Soviet Ruling Class* (New York, 1984). An early work by a keen analyst of Soviet and post-Soviet life is Boris Kagarlitsky, *The Thinking Reed* (London and New York, 1988), with its "partocracy." For more on Machajski, there is the chapter on him in Anthony D'Agostino, *Marxism and the Russian Anarchists* (San Francisco, 1977), and also Marshall Shatz, *Machajski: A Radical Critic of the Russian Intelligentsia and Socialism* (Pittsburgh, 1989). In this vein is Max Nomad, *Aspects of Revolt* (New York, 1959), one of several entertaining books by a Machajski disciple attacking the foibles of the left. The once fashionable idea that the managerial stratum actually ran Soviet Russia was nicely punctured by Jeremy Azrael, *Managerial Power and Soviet Politics* (Cambridge, MA, 1966).

CHAPTER 12

Stalin's foreign policy may be followed in Jonathan Haslam, *The Soviet Union and the Struggle for Collective Security in Europe, 1933–1939* (New York, 1984). Foreign policy was not Stalin's métier, thinks Haslam, so he left things to Litvinov. Haslam carefully traces the errors and misconceptions in Western policy. Jiri Hochman, *The Soviet Union and the Failure of Collective Security, 1934–1938* (Ithaca, 1984) takes the opposite view, that Stalin was looking for a pact with the Nazis all along. Robert Tucker, *Stalin in Power: The Revolution from Above, 1928–1941* (New York, 1990) follows Hochman for the most part. My own view is in Anthony D'Agostino, *Soviet Succession Struggles* (Boston and London, 1988), a fuller account than this chapter. Silvio Pons, *Stalin and the Inevitable War, 1936–1941* (London, Frank Cass, 2002), using Soviet archives, suggests Stalin's "cultural Bolshevism" is the key to his policy, at any rate his presumed *realpolitik* in the phrases of "capitalist encirclement." Geoffrey Roberts, *The Soviet Union and the Origins of the Second World War: Russo-German Relations and the Road to War, 1933–1941* (New York, 1995) is closer to Haslam and finds the Soviets still available to Britain until summer 1939. Michael Jabara Carley, *1939: The Alliance That Never Was and the Coming of World War Two* (Chicago, 1999) is a close study of attitudes toward Russia and takes a view similar to Roberts and Haslam. Gerhard Weinberg, *Germany and the Soviet Union, 1939–1941* (London, 1954), is still worth reading. On the death of Trotsky, Victor Serge and Natalia Sedova Trotsky, *The Life and Death of Leon Trotsky* (New York, 1975), is a fascinating memoir. Most recent is Bertrand Patenaude, *Trotsky: Downfall of a Revolutionary* (New York, 2010). The controversies surrounding Stalin's failure to react to warnings in 1941 and the thesis of a presumed preemptive strike by Russia are given a thorough and satisfying review by Gabriel Gorodetsky, *Grand Delusion, Stalin and the German Invasion of Russia* (New Haven, 1999).

CHAPTER 13

The literature on the war in Russia does not form a prominent part of the voluminous literature on World War II, but it is still vast. Most who have written on it have begun with the journalism of Alexander Werth, so it makes sense for the student to begin there as well, with *Russia at War* (New York, 1964). The latest overview is Geoffrey Roberts, *Stalin's Wars: From World War to Cold War, 1939–1953* (New Haven, 2006). For military history, there are the many writings of David Glantz, of which perhaps the most pertinent to this account is *Colossus Reborn: The Red Army at War, 1941–1943* (Lawrence, KA, 2005). Still valuable is John Erickson, *The Road to Stalingrad* (New York, 1975), along with his other works on the subject. Richard

Overy, *Russia's War* (London, 1998), stresses that the outcome could not be predicted before Stalingrad. Many legends are updated and some discarded in Catherine Merridale, *Ivan's War: The Red Army, 1939–1945* (London, 2005). Mark Harrison, *Soviet Planning in Peace and War* (Cambridge, 1985), finds that the Germans had a slight edge in 1942 and the Soviets a slight edge thereafter, as much because of artful improvising as anything else. Nikolai Voznesensky, *The War Economy of the USSR in the Period of the Great Patriotic War* (Moscow, 1948), is the classic account of the eastward transfer of industry by the head of the wartime *gosplan*, later shot by Stalin in 1949. For the Nazi policies and the triumph of ruthless colonization over psychological warfare, see Alexander Dallin, *German Rule in Russia, 1941–1945* (New York, 1957). Interviews with the German generals are in B. H. Liddell Hart, *The German Generals Talk* (New York, 1948); the Russian generals' memoirs are excerpted in Seweryn Bailer (ed.), *Stalin and His Generals* (New York, 1969).

CHAPTER 14

Historians have told much of the story of the revolution by means of biographies of the individual leaders. Stalin biography's foundation stone is Boris Souvarine, *Staline, aperçu historique du bolchévisme* (1936), translated as *Stalin: a Critical Survey of Bolshevism* (New York, 1939). Although no one knew Stalin better than he, Trotsky said that Souverine's book was useful to him for his own unfinished 1940 biography, *Stalin: an Appraisal of the Man and His Influence* (New York, 1967). The question of Stalin's necessity was introduced by Isaac Deutscher, *Stalin: A Political Biography* (Oxford, 1949). This was followed by his three-volume Trotsky biography: *The Prophet Armed, Trotsky, 1879–1921* (New York and London, 1954); *The Prophet Unarmed: Trotsky, 1921–1929* (London and New York, 1959); and *The Prophet Outcast: Trotsky, 1929–1940* (London and New York, 1963). Among Deutscher's many critics none was so sharp as Julius Jacobson, whose views can be found in *Soviet Communism and the Socialist Vision* (New Brunswick, NJ, 1972). Deutscher's material came mainly from the Trotsky Archive and Trotsky Exile Archive at Harvard. Now we have Dmitri Volkogonov, *Stalin: Triumph and Tragedy* (London, 1992) and the more unorthodox Edvard Radzinsky, *Stalin* (New York, 1996), using Soviet archive material. Stalin the revolutionary war lord is stressed in Kevin McDermott, *Stalin: Revolutionary in an Era of War* (New York, 2006). Alec Nove's *Was Stalin Really Necessary?* (London, 1964) contains his original 1962 *Encounter* article with that title along with other essays exploring the rationality or lack thereof in Soviet planning. In the same vein is Peter Wiles, "The Importance of Being Djugashvili," *Problems of Communism* (Summer 1964). For the Russian revolution as one of a number of modernizing projects, see Theodore Von Laue, *The World Revolution of Modernization: The Twentieth Century in Global Perspective* (New York, 1987). Communism as a phase in the Russian state narrative is the theme of Nicolai Berdyaev, *The Origin of Russian Communism* (Ann Arbor, 1960), one of a number of influential writings by a leading religious philosopher, already cited above. The quotations of the characters of Thomas Mann, Settembrini and Naphta, are from *The Magic Mountain* (New York, 1952), pp. 399 and 404. My own views on the glasnost debate about Stalinism are in Anthony D'Agostino, *Gorbachev's Revolution, 1985–1991* (Basingstoke and New York, 1998). A. A. Danilov et al., *The History of Russia: The Twentieth Century* (Heron Press, n. p., 1996) has a contemporary Russian assessment of the rationality of Stalinism. A Western view is Geoff Eley, *Forging Democracy: The History of the Left in Europe, 1850–2000* (Oxford and New York, 2002).

Index

About the Author

ANTHONY D'AGOSTINO is the author of several books, including *Soviet Succession Struggles* and *Gorbachev's Revolution, 1985–1991*, as well as articles and reviews in many journals, including *American Historical Review*, *Journal of the Historical Society*, *Survey* (London), *Slavic Review*, *Russian Review*, and *Journal of Cold War Studies*. He contributes to H-DIPLO, History News Network, and Johnson's Russia List. Over the years, he has made more than 100 radio and television appearances.